Churchill

by his granddaughter, Celia Sandys

[signature: Celia Sandys]

IMPERIAL WAR MUSEUM

Published by the Imperial War Museum
Lambeth Road, London, SE1 6HZ

© Trustees of the Imperial War Museum 2005
Text © Celia Sandys 2005

ISBN 1 904897 22 3

Printed in the UK by Butler & Tanner, Frome and London
Designed by James Campus

This book is adapted from *Churchill* by Celia Sandys,
published by Contender Books in 2003.

Frontispiece: Winston Churchill *by Sir William Orpen, 1916*

CONTENTS

FOREWORD

'I felt as though I were walking with destiny, and that all my past life had been but a preparation for this hour and this trial.'

These were my grandfather's thoughts on becoming Prime Minister on 10 May 1940.

What would have happened if Winston Churchill had not been called to lead his country in its darkest hour? Without him who would have mobilised the English language and sent it into battle? Who else could have offered 'Blood, toil, tears and sweat' to such an effect?

Without Winston Churchill the world we live in today would be a very different place.

I am honoured and delighted to have been asked to write this companion book to the Churchill Museum and to be associated with this magnificent exhibition which, using iconic objects and images and an array of interactive technology, takes us on a fascinating journey of discovery through the life of Britain's wartime leader.

I hope that this book will prove to be a worthy reminder of the inspiring story of the extraordinary man whom I am proud to have called Grandpapa.

1

YOUNG CHURCHILL 1874–1900

Winston Leonard Spencer Churchill was born at Blenheim Palace on 30 November 1874. The British Empire was at the height of its power. Queen Victoria was on the throne and would still be Queen when the new baby was first elected to Parliament 25 years on.

While Britain governed vast areas of the world, the rest of Europe was anxiously watching the rise of Germany, the menace of which would play a large part in the long life of the new baby. America, with which Churchill would develop a close affinity, although benefiting in brawn and brain from the great immigration from Europe, was still many years from becoming a world power.

This was the Victorian age of gaslight and candles. There were no motorcars, only horse drawn vehicles and steam trains. The telephone had yet to be invented. Medicine was basic. Child mortality meant that one child in six did not live to its first birthday.

Winston Churchill was born into a family which had already made history. Through his father, Lord Randolph Churchill, he was descended from John Churchill, Queen Anne's Captain General. In recognition of his military

Young Winston, boasting the red hair which he passed on to subsequent generations of his family.

victories she had created him the first Duke of Marlborough in 1702 and soon after funded the building of Winston's birthplace, Blenheim Palace.

Winston's mother was a beautiful American, Jennie Jerome. She was the daughter of Leonard Jerome, a man who pursued a variety of interests in expansive style – publishing, yachting, the opera and racing. Largely brought up in Paris, Jennie met Lord Randolph at a ball on board HMS *Ariadne* at Cowes. She was 19, he 24. It was love at first sight and they were married at the British Embassy in Paris seven months later on 15 April 1874.

At the time of his birth none of Winston's British ancestors since the first Duke of Marlborough had made any significant mark in the nation's affairs and, although Lord Randolph would soon become a popular politician, the family history did not suggest that the baby would become the man of the millennium at the end of the next century. His American ancestry through Jennie included the entrepreneurial talents of her father and a great-grandmother who was said to be an Iroquois Indian. The mixture of British and American blood in the baby Winston was to

Churchill's ancestor, the first Duke of Marlborough, was Queen Anne's most distinguished general. The family home, Blenheim Palace, was paid for by a grateful nation and named after his most famous victory.

Blenheim Palace

As a reward for her Captain General's successful campaigns, Queen Anne presented John Churchill, First Duke of Marlborough, with the Royal Manor of Woodstock. He was also given a grant to build Blenheim Palace, named after his most famous battle. He commissioned the renowned architect John Vanbrugh to create one of the grandest houses in England, which was eventually completed in 1725, three years after its owner's death.

Churchill said that he had taken two important decisions at Blenheim – to be born and to get married – and he never regretted either. Although his father, as the younger son, would never own Blenheim, young Winston spent many holidays here with his grandparents. He proposed to Clementine Hozier in the Temple of Diana where, during an afternoon walk in the grounds of the Palace, they had taken shelter from the rain. At his request he was buried in the local churchyard at Bladon, by the gates of Blenheim.

prove a powerful brew but in what proportions the man of the millennium sprang from his genes, upbringing and luck, readers will decide for themselves as his life unfolds.

The Churchills were a busy couple. Lord Randolph was making his name in politics and Lady Randolph led a hectic social life. Even by upper-class Victorian standards Winston saw little of his parents and it was therefore not surprising that his nanny, Mrs Everest, became his symbol of home. He later wrote, 'My nurse was my confidante. Mrs Everest it was who looked after me and tended all my wants.' As a young man he would be at her bedside when she died in 1895: 'My dearest and most intimate friend during the whole of the 20 years I had lived.'

Lord Randolph, whom Winston idolised, also died in that year. By the time of his death he was a fallen political star and had unfortunately never established a satisfactory relationship with his son for whom there remained 'only to pursue his aims and vindicate his memory.' Winston's dealings with his mother were more rewarding. Although his early memories of Lady Randolph were 'of a fairy princess. I loved her dearly – but at a distance,' he said, by his late teens their relationship would mature into a useful partnership, 'more like brother and sister than mother and son.'

Winston's early schooling was mainly at a quiet school in Brighton where it was hoped the bracing sea air and the proximity of the

Top: *An early picture of baby Winston.*

Above: *Winston's baby rattle.*

family doctor, who lived there, would between them take care of his many ailments. It was a fortunate choice medically as without the doctor's immediate attention it is probable that Winston would have succumbed to the pneumonia he caught in 1886. But the cosy little school was a poor preparation for the more stringent academic standards of Harrow where Winston's mediocre achievements led to the fiction that he was a dunce at school. However, that is a myth which Churchill, in later life, was amused to foster because in reality, when his imagination was captured, his thirst for knowledge was unquenchable.

In his first term at Harrow, while languishing at the bottom of the lowest form, he won a prize open to the whole school by reciting 1,200 lines

Above left: *Churchill's father Lord Randolph Churchill, was the younger son of the 7th Duke of Marlborough and Member of Parliament for Woodstock, the constituency in which the family home, Blenheim Palace, was situated. His mother, Jennie Jerome was a beautiful American who had been educated in Europe. Lord Randolph and Jennie became engaged three days after meeting at a ball.*

Above: *The young Lady Randolph Churchill. One admirer described her as having 'more of the panther than of the woman in her look'.*

of Macaulay's *Lays of Ancient Rome* without a single mistake. It was an early indication of the prodigious memory which would serve him so well in public life. In the school archives is Winston's essay of some 2000 words on an imaginary battle. It foreshadowed the author's subsequent mastery of the English language and feeling for history to such effect that the English master, who could not have predicted the destiny of his pupil, was so impressed with the writing that he preserved it.

Apart from excelling at fencing, in which he won the public schools' championship, Winston was undistinguished both at work and play. But he was by no means unnoticed. By the time he left Harrow he had already developed the characteristics which would ensure he would always be a force to be reckoned with. His private tutor, coaching him for his third attempt to pass the examination for the Royal Military Academy, Sandhurst, complained to Lord Randolph that Winston was 'rather too much inclined to teach his instructors instead of endeavouring to learn from them'. However, he passed and at the beginning of September 1893 began his army career.

With his history of one medical problem after another it was not surprising that Winston, facing the physical rigours of Sandhurst, informed Lady Randolph, 'I am cursed with so feeble a body I can hardly support the fatigues of the day.' His chest measurement was such that he was told it would have to be increased

Lady Randolph Churchill with her two sons, Winston, aged 13, and Jack, 7. Churchill wrote, 'She shone for me like the evening star. I loved her dearly – but at a distance'. After Lord Randolph's death she married twice more and died in 1921, aged 67.

Mrs Everest, young Winston's beloved nanny whom he described as 'my confidante'. Mrs Everest it was who looked after me and tended to all my wants. It was to her I poured out all my many troubles.' On her death he said he had lost 'my dearest and most intimate friend during the whole of the twenty years I had lived.'

Mary Soames
Churchill's daughter

I think he did have a difficult childhood. It was very centred on Mrs Everest, who was his wonderful nanny and great confidante. He writes most movingly about her in *My Early Life*. When he was at school he always longed for her to come down. Much later in life one of his contemporaries said how struck he had been by the fact that young Winston walked down the high street with Mrs Everest on his arm. She was quite an old nanny body, with a bonnet and a shawl, but Winston was so proud of her and paraded her down the high street.

He adored his mother, but she was fairly remote, and his father was probably rather alarming. Certainly as my father got older and into school reports, his father was quite ferocious. My father yearned for his good opinion.

Lord Randolph became convinced that Winston was idle, and not clever. I think in fact that my father was very good at the things he enjoyed and was interested in and extremely bad at the things that bored him. I don't think he's necessarily unique in that.

My father was deeply, deeply, sorrowful when Lord Randolph died. I always remember years and years later, just a few years before he died, I was alone with my father and I asked him, 'Is there anything in your life you feel you've missed?' I thought he would say, 'Yes, I would have liked to win the Victoria Cross' – which I'm sure he would have liked to do – but he said to me without much delay for thought, 'Oh yes. I'd have liked my father to live long enough to see that I was going to be some good.'

before he could pass out as an officer. Dogged by a variety of ailments, a lesser young man would have faltered but Winston never wavered. Writing to his father during his second term he said, 'On Friday they made me come into hospital'. From his bed he was 'reading up a very good work on tactics'.

Lord Randolph invariably compared Winston unfavourably with his brother Jack, six years younger, but the elder brother persisted in the quest for the friendship he had always craved with his father. He was on the point of succeeding when it was decided that Lord Randolph, because of his poor health, should go abroad to try to regain his strength. In June 1894 Winston saw his parents off on the boat train in London, quite unaware he would never again see his father in proper physical or mental health.

Six months later Winston took his final examinations at Sandhurst, having already come second in the riding, beaten by one mark in two hundred for first place. In the written work he passed 20th out of 130. 'The World,' he said, 'opened like Aladdin's Cave. Instead of creeping in at the bottom I passed with honours. I could learn quickly enough the things that mattered.' His father would at last have approved of these achievements had he been better able to understand what was going on around him. Unfortunately he was failing fast from what has since been recognised as a brain tumour, and was brought back to

Above: Winston's first
school report from
St George's School, Ascot.

Right: Winston in Dublin,
aged five.

The Harrow School punishment book: an entry for Winston on 25 May 1891 shows that he received seven strokes of the cane for 'breaking into premises and doing damage.'

England on Christmas Eve 1894. He died on 24 January 1895, 70 years to the day before his son would die.

On 20 February Churchill was commissioned into a fashionable cavalry regiment, the 4th Hussars.

As head of the family the young Churchill found himself burdened with new responsibilities. His father's estate was swallowed by debts, while his mother's private income would not cover her many expenses. His army pay could not possibly establish him as the family breadwinner or sustain him in the political career – Members of Parliament were unpaid in those days – on which he was already set. He lost no time in seeking a remedy for this situation.

Stationed with his regiment at Hounslow on the fringes of London, Churchill was impatient to make an immediate impact, but the active service which he described as the 'swift road to promotion and advancement' seemed unavailable as virtually the whole British army was occupied with the chores and pleasures of peacetime soldiering. However, Churchill was not to be denied. Using his family connections to good effect, and taking advantage of the winter leave granted for the hunting season, he set off for Cuba where a guerrilla war between indigenous rebels and the island's Spanish rulers was reaching a conclusive stage. In his pocket was an introduction to the Spanish Captain-General and a contract with the *London Daily Graphic* for letters from the front.

In later life, Churchill enjoyed perpetuating the myth that he had been a dunce at school. However, although he had no aptitude for maths or the classics, he was soon shown to have a prodigious memory and a passion for the English language and for military history. Here, he is seen in his Harrow uniform, ready to collect a prize.

HARROW SONGS

On 18 December 1940, on the occasion of the school's annual Songs, Churchill visited Harrow, which had recently been bombed. To mark his visit a new verse had been added to *Stet Fortuna Domus*:

> Nor less we praise in sterner days
> The leader of our Nation,
> And CHURCHILL'S name shall win acclaim
> From each new generation.
> While in this fight to guard the Right
> Our country you defend Sir,
> Here grim and gay we mean to stay,
> And stick it to the end, Sir.

When he returned the following year for what had now become established as Churchill Songs, he asked that 'sterner' be substituted for 'darker'.

To celebrate Churchill's eightieth birthday a new verse was added to the song *Forty Years On*:

> Sixty years on – though in time growing older,
> Younger at heart you return to the Hill:
> You who in days of defeat ever bolder,
> Led us to victory, serve Britain still.

And for his ninetieth birthday:

> We who were born in the calm after thunder
> Cherish our freedom to think and to do;
> If in our turn we forgetfully wonder,
> Yet we'll remember we owe it to you.

He crossed the Atlantic to New York where his short stay contributed to his future career at least as much as his subsequent month in Cuba. He was met on the quayside by Congressman Bourke Cockran, an admirer of Lady Randolph. A distinguished lawyer and politician, Cockran was impressed with the vigour of Churchill's language and the breadth of his views as he took the young man around. The two men struck an instant rapport and thereafter maintained a longstanding political correspondence. Cockran was a profound influence upon the young Churchill who wrote of his host's political oratory, 'He was my model. I learned from him how to hold thousands in thrall.'

Churchill arrived in Havana on 20 November. Ten days later, on his 21st birthday, he was in action, a bullet missing his head by a foot before killing the horse behind him. It was the first example of what would be his extraordinary life-long luck in the face of enemy fire. His short foray into a foreign war earned him his first medal, the Spanish Order of Military Merit 1st Class, and £1,250 in today's money, his first income as a journalist. His letters from the front, written while living rough, were a portent of his formidable talents.

Churchill returned to the 4th Hussars in January 1896, nine months before they were due to sail for an eight-year stint in India. He saw this as a political backwater and implored

Although it took him three attempts to pass the entrance exam, Churchill did well at Sandhurst, passing out 20th in his group of 130 in the written examination. In the riding examination he came second, beaten by one mark out of 200.

his mother to pull every string which might lead to 'scenes of adventure and excitement – places where I could gain experience and derive advantage.' Lady Randolph failed and Churchill, assiduously promoted by his mother, used the nine months in England to cultivate important people.

He sailed for India in September 1896. There in the garrison of Bangalore, while others lazed indolently during the hot afternoons, Churchill studied. Recognising the large gaps in his education, he sent home for books. He read widely and voraciously, creating his own university course. The daily studies over, he

In the Fourth Hussars, 1895. The expensive lifestyle expected of an officer in this fashionable cavalry regiment was to prove a drain on the family finances for the next five years.

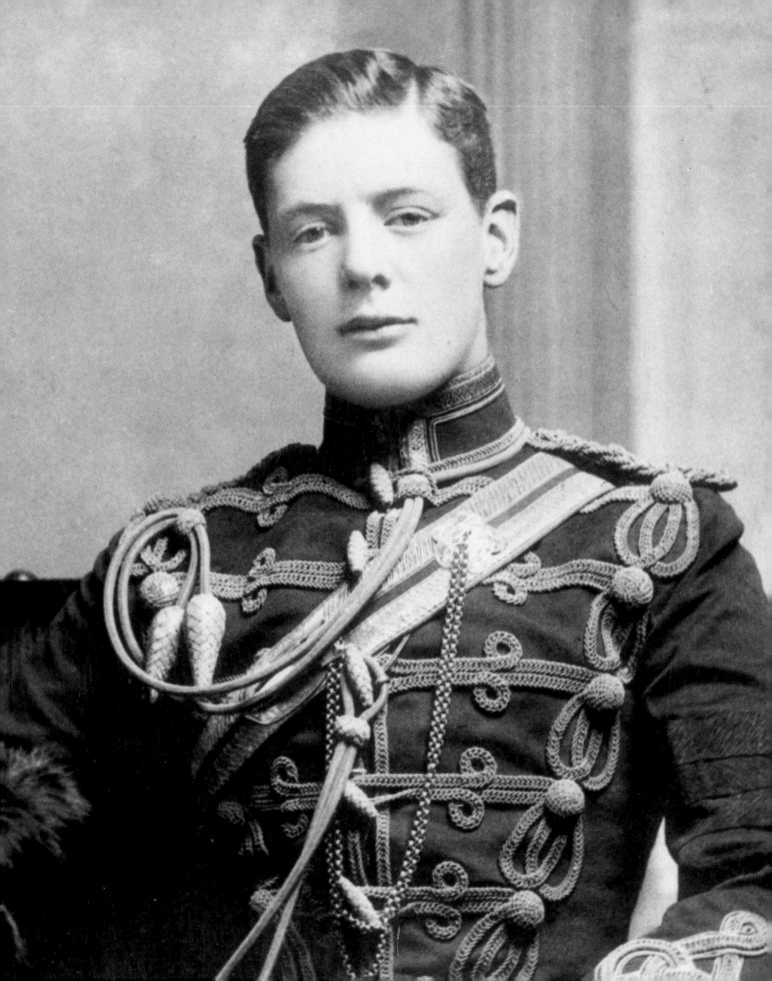

turned out in the early evening for polo, becoming a high handicap player and a permanent member of his regimental team which, in a land where polo was a serious pursuit, won the All India Cup.

It was while at Bangalore, while out riding with a fellow officer, that he first announced his political ambition. Puffing his cigar, (he had acquired the taste while at Sandhurst), he declared that he was giving up the army for politics. But for him it was not the mere achievement of entering Parliament, 'One day I shall be Prime Minister,' he concluded. He was a bumptious and supremely confident young man who did not always endear himself to his companions.

Apart from studies and polo, he had one other diversion from the routine which bored him: Miss Pamela Plowden. Meeting her at a polo match, he wrote immediately to his mother, 'She is the most beautiful girl I have ever known.' The love affair would continue for several years before petering out in the face of Churchill's determination to win the fame and fortune required for launching and funding his political career. He was not a ladies' man. Pamela later said of him, 'The first time you meet Winston you see all his faults, the rest of your life you spend in discovering his virtues'. In the summer of 1897, while in England on leave, Churchill learned of a tribal uprising on the North-West Frontier of India and the formation of the Malakand Field Force to quell the unruly tribesmen. An acquaintance, Major-General Sir Bindon Blood, had been appointed in command. Abandoning his leave, Churchill took the first boat back to India, simultaneously sending a telegram to Blood asking to be appointed to his staff. There was no vacancy immediately available but Churchill persuaded his own colonel to grant him leave. With a commission from an Indian newspaper, the *Pioneer*, and a promise of payment from the *Daily Telegraph*, he set off as a war correspondent to cover the 2,500-mile train journey from Bangalore to the frontier.

Within a month he had replaced an officer killed in action and, while still reporting for his newspapers, had himself been engaged in

Above left: Hyderabad, 1896. Churchill is seated at the far right of the group sitting on the ground.

Below left: Churchill, seated bottom from left, with fellow officers of the 4th Hussars, Bangalore, 1897.

As a subaltern in Bangalore (1896–9). During this time Churchill became a high handicap polo player and a regular member of his regimental team. His undemanding military duties also enabled him to make up for not having had a university education by spending many hours reading classic works of history, economics and philosophy.

Celia Sandys
Churchill's grandaughter

I believe that the turning point in his life was the armoured train ambush. It was as a result of this that he was imprisoned and escaped with a price of £25 on his head for his capture 'Dead or Alive'. Reports of heroic action and his subsequent escape ensured his place on the international stage. Until then he had been his famous father's son. He had been noticed as a young man who was going somewhere, but when he took charge of the armoured train his fame was assured. It was from that moment that everyone noticed what Winston Churchill did and said for the rest of his life.

By the time he got to Durban he had had the most extraordinary month in his life: from the moment of the ambush, through his command of the situation there and his subsequent capture, his dejected march to Pretoria, his escape and all the dangers along the way. After a series of incredible experiences he arrived in Durban to find a huge crowd waiting on the quayside. He was already a confident young man, but his reception must have confirmed his belief that he had something to do in the world.

heavy hand-to-hand fighting. His letters home spared his mother no detail: 'I was close to both officers when they were hit and fired my revolver at a man at 30 yards who tried to cut up poor Hughes's body'. There seems little doubt that he enjoyed the danger, writing to Lady Randolph on another occasion, 'Bullets are not worth considering. Besides I am so conceited I do not think the Gods would create so potent a being for so prosaic an ending.'

His dramatic accounts by no means exaggerated his own performance. General Blood, corresponding with the 4th Hussars' commanding officer back in Bangalore, wrote 'if [Churchill] gets the chance he will have the VC or DSO.' There is no doubt Churchill hoped for such a chance for in his eyes military decorations were to be admired as symbols of courage, which for him was 'the first of human qualities because it guarantees all others.' But he had to make do with a not insignificant mention in despatches. The campaign over, he returned to Bangalore where, in only five weeks, he wrote his first book, *The Malakand Field Force*. Published in March 1898 it was widely regarded as a military classic and earned its author some £30,000 in today's money.

Churchill now began to lobby through his mother for a place in the expedition General

One of Churchill's early opportunities to display his extraordinary courage came when an armoured train on which he was travelling was ambushed and derailed. Ignoring the fact that he was a journalist in the company of soldiers, he took charge, persuaded the frightened engine driver to assist him and was able to salvage the engine and return it, loaded with wounded men to safety. Afterwards, he found himself facing an armed Boer Horseman and was taken prisoner.

Churchill's Literary Legacy

From his early campaigns came *The Malakand Field Force* and *The River War*. These were quickly followed by his only novel, *Savrola*, and a two-volume biography of his father. *The World Crisis* was a six-volume history of the First World War.

Of his later works, *My Early Life*, a memoir published in 1930, is often regarded as his most engaging book. A four-volume biography of his distinguished ancestor, the first Duke of Marlborough, occupied much of his writing time during the 'wilderness' years of the 1930s.

His greatest achievement was *The Second World War*, published in six volumes between 1948 and 1954. He then finished the four-volume *The History of the English-Speaking Peoples*, which he had started in the 1930s, completing a remarkable literary legacy of 40 titles in over 60 volumes. In 1953 he was awarded the Nobel Prize for Literature.

Sir Herbert Kitchener was mounting in the Sudan. The main stumbling block was Kitchener himself, who took exception to Churchill manipulating the system to his own advantage. Churchill succeeded only by invoking the support of Lord Salisbury, the Prime Minister, when presenting him with a copy of *The Malakand Field Force* while on home leave. Permission granted, much to the irritation of the War Office, he set off at his own expense and caught up with the 21st Lancers in Cairo as they were about to leave for the Sudan.

On 2 September 1898 at Omdurman just north of Khartoum, Kitchener's force clashed with thousands of massed Dervish tribesmen. Churchill survived unscathed in a cavalry charge through their midst, although in two minutes the regiment lost a quarter of its strength. Due to an injured shoulder he was wielding a pistol instead of the traditional cavalry sword. 'I saw the gleam of [a Dervish's] sword as he drew it back… I fired two shots into him at about two yards. I saw before me another figure with uplifted sword. I raised my pistol and fired. So close were we that the pistol actually struck him.' Churchill's book of the campaign, *The River War*, published a year later, would become the standard history. Its trenchant criticism of Kitchener's policies after the campaign upset the War Office and led to instructions, which exist to this day, curbing the literary and journalistic freedom of serving soldiers.

Having established that he could earn more by the pen than the sword, Churchill resigned his commission in the Army and stood for Parliament. Narrowly beaten in a by-election at Oldham, he became an obvious choice as a correspondent to cover the war which was about to break out in South Africa, a conflict between British imperialism and Boer nationalism. The *Morning Post* was the highest bidder for his services, settling for some £12,000 a month in today's values and leaving with him the copyright of his reports. Sailing for South Africa, he was the highest paid journalist of the day.

Churchill's (on far right of picture) status as a journalist did not prevent him being treated as a prisoner of war after the 'armoured train' incident in Natal in November 1899.

On 30 October 1899 Churchill disembarked in Cape Town, made time to take up his introduction to the British High Commissioner, Sir Alfred Milner, and set off within 24 hours for the war front in Natal. Plunging into action, he was accompanying three officers and 100 troops on an armoured train when it was ambushed and derailed. Oblivious of the shrapnel shells bursting overhead and the bullets ricocheting from the trucks, Churchill took charge of clearing the wreckage sufficiently for the engine to escape. Loading it with wounded he directed the engine to safety before returning on foot with the intention of shepherding more men away. But the

remainder had already been taken prisoner and, unarmed and held at rifle point, he was also forced to surrender. The wounded carried the story back with them and the British and South African press carried glowing testimonials to Churchill's gallantry.

Taken prisoner on 15 November and incarcerated in Pretoria, he did not remain long in captivity. Late in the evening of 12 December he clambered over the wall and vanished with a price of £25 on his head 'Dead or Alive'. Detractors later variously claimed that he had broken parole and abandoned colleagues who also intended to escape. (In *Churchill Wanted Dead or Alive*, HarperCollins 1999, I have conclusively proved these charges to be unfounded.) Ten days later he knocked on the door of the British Consulate at the port of Lourenço Marques in Portuguese East Africa (now Maputo in Mozambique) having arrived concealed among bales of wool in a railway wagon. During the preceding days he had ridden a freight train, walked many miles, been hidden down a mine shaft by friendly miners, one of whom was Daniel Dewsnap from Oldham where Churchill failed at his first attempt to get into Parliament.

He became a household name when he arrived by overnight boat on 23 December in Durban, the port decked overall in flags to greet him. He addressed the crowd from the steps of the town hall, spent the night with the Governor of Natal and on Christmas Eve was

After escaping from a prisoner-of-war camp in Pretoria, Churchill returned to active service with an unpaid commission in the South African Light Horse, though he continued to earn his living as a journalist.

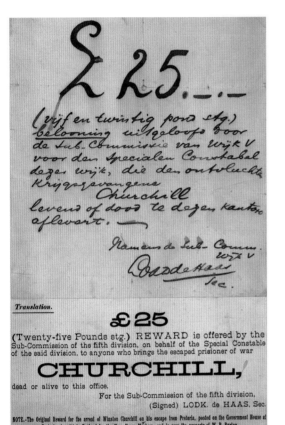

Poster in Afrikaans and English offering a £25 reward for information leading to Churchill's recapture.

Right: revolver lent to Churchill by British mine manager John Howard. Howard and trusted colleagues hid Churchill down a mineshaft for three days, gave him food and whisky, and then smuggled him onto a train to neutral territory.

Below left: *Churchill, (seated second left, middle row) poses with fellow Boer War journalists. Having proved himself with reports from his campaigns in India and the Sudan, he had gone to South Africa as the highest paid war correspondent of his day.*

Bottom: *Churchill triumphant in Durban, with the cowboy hat he had acquired when buying new clothes in Lourenço Marques.*

Churchill the Journalist

Churchill began his writing career for financial reasons, and continued it throughout his life at least in part because he always needed the money. His time in the cavalry, his mother's needs, his political ambitions allied to his lifestyle, his purchase of Chartwell – which Clementine always maintained they could not afford – all made demands on his purse. He resigned from the army when he found that his reports to newspapers and the books resulting from campaigns on the north-west frontier of India and in the Sudan were earning much more than his military salary. In 1899 he became the highest paid journalist of the day, earning £12,000 a month in today's money, plus all expenses, when he went to South Africa as the *Morning Post*'s correspondent for the Boer War. During the next 40 years, in addition to his immense literary output, he would write over 700 articles for newspapers and periodicals in Britain and America.

back with the troops a few yards from where he had been captured less than six weeks previously.

The Commander-in-Chief, General Sir Redvers Buller, offered Churchill a commission in a locally raised regiment, The South African Light Horse. He accepted instantly. It was a regiment of colonialists and gentlemen rankers among whom Churchill 'lived from day to day in perfect happiness'. He accepted no army pay, thus circumventing the War Office ban on journalism prompted by his own earlier literary activities. Enjoying the best of both worlds, war correspondent and soldier, Churchill remained the highest paid journalist and, always plunging into the thick of action, was able to keep the *Morning Post* readers well informed.

His experience over the next few weeks probably influenced his attitude to war as much as his time in the trenches during the First World War. He always moved towards the

sound of gunfire, relishing the excitement and exhilarated by personal danger, but it was in Natal that he first weighed the tragic against the heroic. 'Ah, horrible war, amazing medley of the glorious and the squalid, the pitiful and the sublime, if modern men of light and leading saw your face closer, simple folk would see it hardly ever,' was his verdict to the readers of the *Morning Post*.

His views were expressed plainly. No one needed to read between the lines when he wrote, 'Whatever maybe said of the generals it is certain that all will praise the courage of the regimental officer and the private soldier.' These were not just the words of a spectator or the thoughts of a mere junior officer.

The historian Thomas Pakenham, writing about the fearful battle of Spion Kop, when the generals were overwhelmed by events, described Churchill's intervention in the chain of command, 'instinctively taking over the role of general.' His eager acceptance of wide responsibility was already evident, a characteristic which would often irritate his colleagues.

It was in South Africa, when the campaign in Natal was successfully completed, that Churchill first expressed his policy of magnanimity towards the defeated, writing 'Revenge may be sweet but it is also most expensive.' The establishment in London were outraged and his articles in both British and South African press drew widespread criticism. He was unrepentant. It would take almost half a century, to the end of the Second World War, before such wisdom would become generally accepted.

By mid 1900 the war was virtually won, although, as Churchill had prophesied, the absence of any thought of reconciliation between British and Boer would lead to a further two years of guerrilla warfare. At home a General Election beckoned. Having resigned his commission, Churchill disembarked at Southampton on 20 July 1900.

He returned greatly matured. At the age of 25 he had achieved fame and recognition as

someone whose views commanded respect. He had demonstrated beyond doubt that he could earn his living by his pen. A collection of his dispatches to the *Morning Post* had already sold 13,000 copies and a second collection was to follow. He had established a reputation within the army, many of the officers with whom he had mixed would rise to high command in the First World War when he would be a member of the Cabinet. Some thought him too hot to handle but he would win them over, even Kitchener.

The one thing he had not achieved was the military decoration for bravery which he had so earnestly desired. As a civilian he had been ineligible during the armoured train action and his subsequent escape. Later, as an officer, his conduct in one battle had been characterised by General Ian Hamilton as 'conspicuous gallantry', the language of citations for the Victoria Cross, but the military establishment were not about to decorate a bumptious and egotistical young man who had so often criticised and outsmarted them. He took it philosophically and writing to his brother he concluded, 'I have, however, had a very good puff.'

Celia Sandys
Churchill's grandaughter

As a young man he displayed a total disregard for his own life; it is as though he felt he was invulnerable.

As a child he seemed to have more mishaps than normal, as a teenager he fell from the top of a tree, and soon after that while on a walking tour in Switzerland with Jack and their tutor the boys took a boat out on the lake and decided to have a swim. They got into difficulty and Winston had to swim for his life to get back to the boat, which had been carried away by the wind. He later recalled that he saw 'death staring me in the face'.

There were so many occasions in the first 25 years of his life when he had near-death experiences that it seems incredible that he survived. It was as though there was some sort of magic shield surrounding him and protecting him when danger threatened. Eventually he came to believe in his destiny and that he was being preserved for some special purpose. While in India he wrote to his mother saying, 'Bullets mean nothing to me. I can't believe that the gods would have created so potent a being for so prosaic an ending.'

Churchill in 1899, during his time as a war correspondent in South Africa for the Morning Post.

2

MAVERICK POLITICIAN 1900–29

Churchill wasted no time in opening his election campaign. Parliament was dissolved on 17 September 1900 and two days later he arrived in Oldham in a procession of ten carriages to address an overflowing Theatre Royal. When he described his escape from Pretoria and mentioned the Oldham miner, Daniel Dewsnap, who had helped him, the crowd shrieked: 'His wife's in the gallery!' Whereupon the mill girls burst forth with the new music hall ditty

You've heard of Winston Churchill
This is all I need to say –
He's the latest and the greatest
Correspondent of the day.

The election was fought solely on the issue of the war in South Africa. The Liberal opposition argued that it could have been avoided by more skilful diplomacy and accused the Conservatives of mismanagement in its conduct. Churchill, standing as a Conservative, took the view that it was a just war which should be fought to an indisputable conclusion and followed by a generous settlement. The election was spread over three weeks with Oldham being one of the first constituencies to

vote. When, on 1 October, Churchill was successful, he found himself in great demand to speak in support of candidates still campaigning. Arthur Balfour, soon to become Prime Minister, begged Churchill to speak for him in Manchester. 'After this,' Churchill wrote, 'I never addressed any but the greatest meetings, five or six thousand electors'.

He made his maiden speech in Parliament on 18 February 1901, only four days after taking his seat. The Conservative Party had been returned to government and the debate was on their conduct of the war in South Africa. Churchill advocated a policy of stick and carrot, with leniency towards those Boers who surrendered. His statement, 'If I were a Boer fighting in the field – and if I were a Boer I hope I should be fighting in the field... 'did not endear him to some of his own party but the Conservative press liked both the content and the manner of delivery. The *Daily Express* described it as 'spell binding', while the *Daily Telegraph* referred to his 'lively gestures' and 'sparkling sentences'.

Churchill would never be a party politician. There would be occasions when, for the sake of party discipline, he would allow his own

Campaigning in Manchester, April 1908. Churchill had just been given his first Cabinet post – President of the Board of Trade – and, in accordance with the law in those days, had to return to his constituency to seek re-election. The citizens of Manchester rejected him in favour of the Conservative candidate, and Churchill was forced to await a by-election for the safe Liberal sear of Dundee before returning to the House of Commons. He was out of Parliament for less than three weeks.

Reviving " a certain splendid memory."

Above: *Winston Churchill MP. Elected as Conservative Member of Parliament for Oldham in 1900, Churchill crossed the floor to the Liberals in 1904.*

personal ideas to be subordinated to party policy, but never on fundamental issues. As circumstances changed he would adapt with them, changing his party rather than his principles. He would soon be seen as a reformist, a champion of minorities, and an aristocrat who defended the underdog. He even favoured some measures with a socialistic flavour, such as the nationalisation of railways and the reform of the House of Lords, but the thought of a socialist state was repugnant to him. His instinct in a crisis was for Coalition Government. Thus he began as a Conservative, became a Liberal, was a member of the wartime Coalition Government – as Chancellor of the Duchy of Lancaster in 1915 and then as

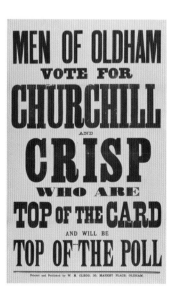

MEN OF OLDHAM
VOTE FOR
CHURCHILL
AND
CRISP
WHO ARE
TOP OF THE CARD
AND WILL BE
TOP OF THE POLL

Minister of Munitions from 1917. He was a member of the post First World War Coalition Government, and returned to the Conservative Party where he was Chancellor of the Exchequer 1924–1929. He lingered in the wilderness until the outbreak of war when, to popular acclaim, he was recalled as First Lord of the Admiralty. This characteristic of following his own compass became apparent when, within three months of his maiden speech, Churchill shocked his own party leaders by attacking the government's proposals for increasing expenditure on the army. He pointed out that although the army as it stood could deal with colonial wars, it could never be expanded sufficiently to take on the great European powers. So what was the point? British power and prosperity depended on the Royal Navy.

Churchill's divergence of thought from his party colleagues continued. During 1901 he and a group of like-minded young Conservatives, called the Hughligans after one of their number, Lord Hugh Cecil, dined each Thursday in the House of Commons, inviting a distinguished guest to join them. That autumn, protesting against the execution of a Boer commandant by the military authorities, Churchill castigated the government and publicly called for an end to the war. In January 1902, to a Conservative audience in Blackpool, he spoke about poverty in Britain and those who had 'only the workhouse or

prison' as alternatives. He toyed with the notion of a National Party free from 'the sordid selfishness of Toryism and the blind appetites of the Radical masses' and took soundings from such senior politicians as the former Liberal Prime Minster, Lord Rosebery. At 27, a Member of Parliament for less than two years, Churchill had become the restless and contro-versial figure he would remain for his long political life.

There were many issues on which Churchill voted against his party. Against the employ-ment of cheap Chinese labour in South Africa and for the legal rights of trades unions were two typical cases, but it was free trade which created the deepest divide between him and his party's leaders. In 1903 the Colonial Secretary, Joseph Chamberlain, proposed a tariff on foreign trade in order to stimulate trade from the Empire and strengthen its bonds with the 'Mother Country'. Churchill saw that handicapping foreign competition would lower standards and raise prices. He organised a Free Trade League saying that the govern-ment's policy would mean 'dear food for the masses and cheap labour for the millionaire'. Churchill was steadily distancing himself further from the Conservative Party.

The following year he decided to stand at the next election as a Liberal, North-West Manchester having chosen him as their candidate. Speaking to his future constituents he declared, 'We want a government that will

Churchill, 1904.

think a little more about the toiler at the bottom of the mine and little less about the fluctuations of the share market in London'. On 31 May Churchill crossed the floor of the House to take his seat on the Liberal opposition benches. In another twenty years, when the Liberals were a spent force, he would return to the Conservative fold but it would not be until the Second World War that the Conservative Party forgave what they saw as treachery, and then only because the country recognised it could no longer do without him.

Balfour resigned in 1905, the Conservative Party split on the issue of tariffs and in disarray. The King sent for Sir Henry Campbell-Bannerman, the Liberal leader, to form a government. Churchill was offered the position of Financial Secretary to the Treasury but persuaded the new Prime Minister to appoint him instead to what was, nominally, a less significant position, Under-Secretary of State for the Colonies. It was a clever move by Churchill for, with the Secretary of State, Lord Elgin, in the House of Lords and inclined to be easy going, the limelight would fall on the Under-Secretary as he took centre stage piloting business through the House of Commons. Lord Elgin would later admit in a letter to his successor that, with Churchill as his Under-Secretary, 'the strain has often been severe'.

Churchill's preoccupations with politics had not kept him from the literary activities on which his income depended. His biography of his father Lord Randolph Churchill was published in 1906 and immediately attracted widespread acclaim. Churchill's own difficulties with party politics were reflected in the conclusion he drew from his father's life: 'The Conservatives, whose forces he so greatly strengthened, the Liberals, some of whose finest principles he notably sustained, must equally regard his life and work with mixed feelings'.

As much as anything it was the lifestyle which Churchill had adopted which enabled

Left: *During the 1909 Parliamentary summer recess Churchill attended German army manoeuvres at the invitation of Kaiser Wilhelm II.*

Right: *Never one to take a holiday unless combined with work, as Colonial Under-Secretary, spent the four months of the 1907–8 parliamentary recess touring East Africa. Here, he arrives at Mombassa Station, Kenya.*

him to accomplish so much over such a varied field of activity. In addition to his constant political activity he would, in his lifetime, write more than forty books and receive the Nobel Prize for Literature, paint over five hundred pictures and be made an honorary Royal Academician, produce a constant stream of journalism, landscape his estate at Chartwell and personally lay the bricks for the cottages and kitchen garden there, yet have time for long meals with interesting guests. He was

never idle. Holidays were not what most people would consider a holiday, they were simply a change of venue which, together with his constantly changing activities, fuelled his unflagging energy.

Budget Day, April 1910: Home Secretary Winston Churchill walks to the House of Commons with the Chancellor of the Exchequer, his friend and mentor David Lloyd George. They are accompanied by Mrs Lloyd George and the Chancellor's Private Secretary.

David Lloyd George

(1st Earl Lloyd George of Dwyfor, OM)

David Lloyd George was born on 17 January 1863. His father died a year later and he was brought up by his uncle, a shoemaker in North Wales. Having been articled to a firm of solicitors he opened his own law practice at the age of 21 and acquired a reputation as a lawyer prepared to defend those pursued by authority. A wonderful orator, in 1890 he was elected as a Liberal to Parliament where he became an active social reformer.

In 1904 Churchill, on leaving the Conservatives for the Liberals, crossed the floor of the House and took his seat beside Lloyd George. Within a few years the two, as members of Herbert Asquith's glittering cabinet, became known as 'the Heavenly Twins of Social Reform', introducing far reaching measures which, in Lloyd George's words, 'lifted the shadow of the workhouse from the homes of the poor'.

Reluctant to approve Britain's entry in the First World War, Lloyd George demanded more vigorous prosecution of the war once hostilities had begun. His impressive performance as Minister of Munitions made him the obvious choice in 1916 to succeed Asquith as Prime Minister when the latter's leadership was seen to be failing. Churchill served under him, as Minister of Munitions, Secretary of State for War and Air and Colonial Secretary.

Lloyd George's Coalition Government lasted until 1922 when he was ousted from power by the Conservatives in his cabinet. An outstanding politician and a master of intrigue he fully justified his nickname 'The Welsh Wizard'. He remained a Member of Parliament until created Earl Lloyd George of Dwyfor in 1945 but died shortly after without ever taking his seat in the House of Lords. In Churchill's words, 'As a man of action, resource and creative energy he stood, when at his zenith, without a rival'.

In the same year as the publication of *Lord Randolph Churchill*, a General Election returned the Liberal Party to power with an overwhelming majority thus setting the stage for Churchill's rapid political advancement. For him the conciliation of South Africa, involving the framing of constitutions for the Transvaal and Orange Free State, was an early political triumph. He was anxious that the new constitutions should be 'the gift of England' and not the outcome of party politics. His aim – responsible and democratic self-government for South Africa – was achieved through a series of parliamentary speeches which were models of clarity and persuasive argument. The process took a year, the Transvaal constitution being promulgated in December 1906 and that of the Orange Free State following in June 1907. King Edward VII, who had followed Churchill's career with interest, wrote to congratulate him: 'His Majesty is glad to see that you are becoming a reliable minister and above all a serious politician which can only be attained by putting country before party'.

This was a welcome letter for Churchill as it was well known that the King, earlier in the year, had been displeased over his part in a Parliamentary debate. The former High Commissioner in South Africa, Lord Milner, had been accused of allowing the unlawful flogging of Chinese labourers. The Conservative opposition, who had been in government at the time, spoke strongly in defence of

Milner. Churchill, who had taken it upon himself to speak for the government, argued that Parliament should condemn the practice but refrain from censuring individuals. Put to the vote, Churchill's view prevailed. He had parried the accusation but in so doing had, once more, drawn on his head the wrath of the Conservative Party and stoked the fury of the Tory press. These hatreds would rankle for years. It would have been better had he left the matter to a more senior government figure, but it was not in his nature to lurk below the parapet.

While Colonial Under-Secretary, Churchill travelled through East Africa, landing at Mombassa and returning through the Sudan and Egypt. He was away from London for four months, on the way out attending the German army manoeuvres as a guest of the Kaiser. (In spite of his ministerial responsibilities Churchill remained a major in a yeomanry regiment, the Queen's Own Oxfordshire Hussars, attended their annual camps and visited the German, French and British armies' manoeuvres.)

The trip produced another book, *My African Journey*, a travelogue leavened with political and economic discussion. A whole chapter pondered the question of racial tensions many years before they arose. He saw the economic potential of the land but 'It is no good,' he wrote, 'trying to lay hold of Tropical Africa with naked fingers'. He put the case for 'Cheap

power not cheap labour,' and he saw this could be achieved if the Nile began its journey by 'leaping through a turbine'. Half a century later, Queen Elizabeth II, inaugurating the Owen Falls Scheme, telegraphed Churchill, then Prime Minister for the second time: 'Your vision has become a reality'.

Vision was one of the characteristics that put Churchill head and shoulders above his colleagues and in 1908, when he became President of the Board of Trade, he began to focus it in earnest on the problems of British society. A member, at only 33, of what was perhaps the most glittering Cabinet in parliamentary history, his relative youth did not

In 1910 Churchill became the youngest Home Secretary since Robert Peel nearly a century earlier. Here he is inspecting Boy Scouts and the Boy's Brigade.

Rising politician Winston Churchill becomes engaged to Clementine Hozier in 1908. Their partnership was to last until his death 57 years later.

Opposite: *Mr and Mrs Churchill ride in splendour during the Coronation of King George V, 22 June 1911.*

Mary Soames
Churchill's daughter

My parents first met at a ball at Crewe House. Winston arrived rather late, the ball was in full swing, and across the room as he came in he saw standing in a doorway this most beautiful girl. His mother was already there and he went up to her and asked, 'Who is that ravishing girl?' So Lady Randolph, good mother, trotted off and came back and said, 'That's Clementine Hozier and it's such a coincidence because Blanche Hozier and I used to be great friends'.

So Lady Randolph brought Winston up to Clementine and introduced him, saying, 'I know your mother quite well, and this is my son Winston,' whereupon my mother, I suppose, thought that Winston would either ask her to dance or talk to her, but instead he stood glued to the floor, simply staring at her. She felt very uncomfortable and he made no conversation at all, so she signalled to a beau of hers standing nearby; he came and asked her to dance and whisked her away. So my mother did not form a favourable impression of him then.

They met again four years later at a dinner party in Clementine's great-aunt's house. Clementine had been asked at the last minute because somebody had dropped out, and she didn't really want to go, she was exhausted and she hadn't got a clean pair of white gloves. But her mother said, 'You must go to Aunt Mary St Helier's, she has been extremely kind to you, so you must help her out'. So she went and when she sat down at dinner there was an empty place to her right because needless to say my father was late – he hadn't really wanted to go either, but had been chased there by his Private Secretary, who said, 'You must go to Lady St Helier's party'.

So he sat down next to Clementine Hozier, and this time he did not miss his chance, and they were engaged a few months later.

inhibit him. In concert with David Lloyd George, the Chancellor, Churchill introduced legislation which began to transform society. 'The unemployed artisan, the casual labourer, the sweated or infirm worker, the worker's widow, the underfed child, the untrained, the undisciplined and exploited boy labourer,' were all to benefit.

Labour exchanges were set up throughout the country to cope with the discontent caused by widespread unemployment; in an evolved form they exist today. He proposed unemployment insurance – 'the dole' – although it would not be introduced until after Churchill had moved on. He established minimum wages covering some 200,000 workers. An advocate always for conciliation, Churchill set up a Standing Court of Arbitration which allowed government to play a more positive part in the settling of differences between capital and labour. None of these measures would excite attention today except by their absence but at the time they were well beyond the expectations of even the Fabian Society, the Socialist organisation that was dedicated to improving conditions for the poor.

Well established in his political career, Churchill was now ready for marriage. In Clementine Hozier he was lucky to find the perfect match. Four years earlier, in 1904, he had asked to be introduced to her at a dance. Gauche and with no small talk, he had not invited her to have supper with him or even to

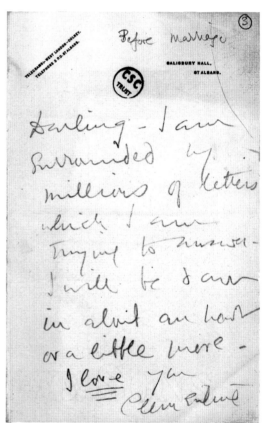

Left: *Winston and Clementine watching army manoeuvres at Aldershot, 1910.*

Right: *Note from Clementine to Churchill declaring love, before their marriage in 1908.*

dance and, in desperation, she had beckoned for someone to rescue her. Their second meeting was at a dinner party in March 1908. Dinner had begun by the time he arrived but from the moment he took his place at the table beside Clementine, he devoted all his attention to his beautiful dining companion, much to the chagrin of Lady Lugard, in whose honour the dinner was, on his other side.

Churchill and Clementine met again a month later after which he wrote to her saying what a pleasure it had been to meet 'a girl with so much intellectual quality and such strong reserves of noble sentiment'. He continued by hoping that, 'We shall meet again and come to

know each other better and like each other more'. This they did and the couple were married at St Margaret's, Westminster, the parish church of the House of Commons, on 12 September 1908. Liberal by inclination, Clementine would be ever his champion but not hesitate to tell him in forthright terms whenever she thought he was making a mistake. Their first child, Diana, was born the following year, followed over the next thirteen

by Randolph, Sarah, Marigold – who died as a young child – and Mary. Busy as he invariably was, Churchill was a family man who would always try to find time to lavish on his children the attention he had been denied as a child.

On becoming Home Secretary in 1910, Churchill's zeal found new outlets. Prison Reform was foremost among these. Within a week of becoming Home Secretary he attended the opening night of Galsworthy's play *Justice*, taking with him the Chairman of the Prisons Commission, Sir Evelyn Ruggles-Brise. Having a sceptical view of the value of prison as either a deterrent to crime or a process of reformation, Churchill sought to reduce the numbers in gaol. His drive to deal with young persons, debtors, drunks and those with short sentences by means other than locking them up, led to a dramatic fall in the prison population. For the remainder he saw that prison conditions were improved.

One of the responsibilities devolving upon the Home Secretary was that of the coal mines where the dangers were such that one in twenty miners would not survive a full working life. Within four months of taking office, Churchill introduced the Coal Mines Bill in Parliament. Mine owners were made to implement comprehensive safety measures and the miners given an eight-hour working day. Boys under fourteen were not to be employed below ground.

The benefits to miners that flowed from the

Clementine Churchill

Clementine Churchill was born Clementine Hozier on 1 April 1885. Her mother, Lady Blanche Hozier, was the eldest daughter of the 10th Earl of Airlie and the wife of Colonel Henry Hozier. The Hoziers did not have a happy marriage and Lady Blanche is known to have had a number of lovers.

It is generally accepted that Clementine's father was either Bertram Mitford – the first Lord Redesdale and grandfather of the famous Mitford sisters – or William George 'Bay' Middleton a dashing army officer and steeplechaser.

Clementine, the second of Lady Blanche's four children, grew up in the shadow of her parents' unhappy marriage and, following a wrangle for custody, eventually lived with her mother first in London then Seaford and Dieppe. Following the death of her eldest daughter Kitty in 1900, Lady Blanche returned to England with her family and Clementine attended Berkhamstead School for Girls. Despite extremely straightened circumstances, Lady Blanche made sure that her daughters received a good education. Clementine was a good linguist and as a result of private lessons and visits to France and Germany she became fluent in both languages. She first met Winston Churchill in 1904 but he did not make a good impression. They met again in March 1908, became engaged in April and were married in September. Diana was born in 1909, Randolph in 1911, Sarah in 1914, Marigold in 1918 (she died in 1921) and Mary in 1922.

Herbert Asquith
1st Earl of Oxford

Churchill, who had been a member of Asquith's cabinet for seven years, wrote of him: 'Mr Asquith was probably one of the greatest peace-time Prime Ministers we have ever had. His intellect, his sagacity, his broad outlook and civic courage maintained him at the highest eminence of public life. But in war he had not those qualities of resource and energy, of prevision and assiduous management, which ought to reside in the executive'.

Herbert Asquith was born in 1852. Educated at Balliol College, Oxford, he became a barrister at 24 and a Member of Parliament ten years later. In opposition for his first six years in the House of Commons, he became Home Secretary in Gladstone's Liberal government of 1892, a position he retained until the Conservatives returned to power three years later.

In 1905, with the Liberals again in government, now under Sir Henry Campbell-Bannerman, he was appointed Chancellor of the Exchequer until becoming Prime Minister on Campbell-Bannerman's resignation in 1908. As Prime Minister he saw through a series of social reforms including the Old Age Pensions Act and the People's Budget which resulted in a conflict with the House of Lords. In 1911 Asquith introduced the Parliament Act aimed at reducing the powers of the Lords in that they would no longer be able to prevent the passage of 'money bills' and would be restricted in their ability to delay other legislation to three sessions of Parliament. He forced this legislation through the Lords when the Conservative opposition gave way in the face of King George V's agreement to Asquith's proposal for the creation of enough Liberal peers to out-vote the Conservatives in the Lords.

On the outbreak of the First World War, Asquith at first resisted proposals to form a coalition government but in May 1915 this measure became inevitable. The Conservatives continued to question Asquith's abilities as a wartime leader and in December 1916 Lloyd George became Prime Minister having collaborated with the opposition to force him to resign.

Asquith did not again hold ministerial office. He lost his seat in the 1918 General Election but was returned again in 1920. He died in 1928 having been made the Earl of Oxford three years before.

Coal Mines Bill were unfortunately not matched by those Churchill intended for shop workers. The Shops Bill was intended to provide such things as time off during the working day, Sunday closing, a half-day holiday each week, proper lighting and lavatory facilities. The shopkeepers' powerful lobby ensured that the only measures to survive Parliament were the imposition of one early closing day a week and the requirement for a meal break during the working day. Although it had nothing to do with his responsibilities as Home Secretary, Churchill also steered through the provisions for unemployment insurance on which he had worked while at the Board of Trade.

He took the widest view of his cabinet responsibilities, offering his views, whether solicited or not, on any subject which he thought needed airing, in the process not infrequently infuriating his colleagues. Thus, when Germany began to threaten European stability, he composed and circulated a remarkable document which forecast the political alignments at the outbreak of the First World War, still three years in the future, and charted the first five weeks of the battle in Belgium and France with remarkable accuracy.

Each day the Home Secretary was required to write a parliamentary report of government business for the King. Churchill's reaction to this task tells us much about him. Most would have been dismayed to be faced with such an

Churchill's visit to Sidney Street led to his having to give evidence at the inquest into the death of the Latvian immigrants involved in the notorious 'siege'. His personal involvement caused widespread criticism and added weight to the arguments of those who felt he lacked judgment.

imposition at the end of a busy day, but Churchill approached the task with relish. The letters, each some 500 words in length, were models of parliamentary sketch-writing which reflected not only Churchill's immense respect for the monarchy but his confidence in dealing with it. His opinions, for in his hands the letter was much more than a mere report, were expressed in pithy phrases. King George V, who had succeeded his father in 1910, branded Churchill's views as 'very socialistic' when he was told of proposed corrective institutions for 'tramps and wastrels' and was reminded that 'there are idlers and wastrels at both ends of the social scale'. Churchill's response, ostensibly affronted and argumentative, respectfully

suggested that as he had forfeited the King's confidence someone else should undertake the daily task. This underlined his self-assurance and ensured that the daily report remained in his hands.

Churchill's immense achievements at the Home Office have been overshadowed by the widespread industrial disputes which shook the country during his time there. His actions in restoring law and order were models of good sense and propriety but were misrepresented by political opponents and the slur 'Tonypandy' still lingers today. It was at Tonypandy, in South Wales, that looting and rioting began during a widespread strike of 25,000 miners in November 1910. Troops were

called for but Churchill, on hearing of this, halted them well short of Tonypandy and instead sent Metropolitan Police reinforcements who used nothing more lethal than their rolled up capes in dealing with the situation. Eventually, when the police appeared to be in danger, some troops were deployed but not a shot was fired, the sight of fixed bayonets causing the crowd to disperse. The only casualty was one striker who had been killed in a scuffle before the troops arrived.

The Times criticised Churchill for weakness in holding the troops back in such a volatile situation. The *Manchester Guardian*, took the opposite view, believing he took a courageous

decision which 'in all probability saved many lives'. It seems he got it right. The general public certainly thought so the following year when he authorised the widespread deployment of troops during a wave of dock and railway strikes. During this unrest, troops opened fire at Llanelly when a train was held up by rioters, the driver knocked unconscious and looting had begun. On that occasion four people were killed, but it was Tonypandy which Churchill's critics remembered.

Between Tonypandy and Llanelly came the so called Battle of Sidney Street, which would have passed unnoticed by history had not Churchill become personally involved. A gang of burglars, led by a Russian anarchist known as 'Peter the Painter', had killed three policemen in December 1910 and were tracked to 100 Sidney Street in London's East End on 3 January 1911. From this house they opened fire on the police and Churchill, having authorised the dispatch of a detachment of Scots Guards, characteristically decided to visit the scene. Top hatted and wearing an overcoat with an astrakhan collar he presented a marvellous subject for the photographers. The house burnt down; two bodies were found in the ruins but 'Peter the Painter' had gone and was never seen again.

Churchill's only direct involvement was to order the fire brigade not to fight the fire when the house was seen to be alight, a sensible intervention considering the bullets flying about, but his presence among the police and soldiers attracted considerable criticism. In Parliament Balfour summed up the general feeling, 'He and a photographer were both risking valuable lives. I understand what the photographer was doing, but what was the Right Honourable Gentleman doing?' One answer could have been because Churchill was a man who always led from the front. However, Churchill seemed to acknowledge the justification of Balfour's words when, recounting them in *Thoughts and Adventures*, he concluded 'With this not altogether unjust reflection I may bring the story to an end'.

In 1911 Churchill became First Lord of the Admiralty, the political head of the world's most powerful navy. A few months earlier a German gunboat had appeared off Agadir, in French controlled Morocco, threatening French interests. Britain supported France and the gunboat withdrew but the incident drew attention to the German programme of warship construction. The new First Lord, concerned to deter German aggression by strengthening the British fleet, was faced with considerable dissent. To the opposition from the Conservative Party was added the disquiet of many Liberal Members of Parliament with pacifist tendencies. Churchill had also to win over conservative-minded senior naval officers who, unused to such energy and brashness, were suspicious of his methods and difficult for him to deal with.

*Clementine and Churchill
at Hendon aerodrome, 1914*

Never a committed party man, Churchill favoured coalition government in times of crisis, with the conflict of party politics temporarily abandoned for the greater good. When the First World War broke out, he was an early advocate of coalition, something the Liberal Prime Minister, Herbert Asquith, initially opposed. The catastrophe of the Dardanelles gave the opposition ample chance to attack the government's conduct of the war and Asquith, conscious of the weakness of his position, now proposed a coalition. As part of the deal, the Conservatives, led by Bonar Law, demanded that Churchill pay the price for his alleged mistakes and he suffered the humiliation of being demoted to the post of Chancellor of the Duchy of Lancaster. In the ensuing reshuffle, Lloyd George briefly remained Chancellor of the Exchequer – a post which would traditionally have gone to the opposition leader. Instead, Bonar Law became Colonial Secretary, Lloyd George became Minister of Munitions and Reginald McKenna took his place at the Exchequer.

He tirelessly visited ships, shore establishments and armament factories, interesting himself not only in technicalities but looking also to the welfare of the men involved. He established the Royal Naval Air Service and, in order that he could contribute his own ideas to its development, learned to fly in an age when it was a very risky business. Against the opposition of senior officers he created the Naval War Staff. Seeking advice from Admiral Lord

Fisher, a retired First Sea Lord, he was determined to increase both the firepower and speed of the Fleet. He introduced guns of 15-inch calibre for the battleships then being built. A naval gun of this size had not been built before and, although the experts had confidence in the design, it took courage to run such technical risk. In order to increase the speed of warships he converted the Fleet from coal to oil and ensured a secure supply of fuel oil by carrying through Parliament the Anglo-Persian Oil Convention.

With the Admiralty yacht *Enchantress* at his disposal he could now travel without even the inconvenience of shifting bedrooms. He described her as 'largely my office, almost my home'. He spent so much time afloat while visiting the Fleet, a total of eight months in the three years leading up to the outbreak of war in 1914, that Lloyd George, the Chancellor, chided him: 'You have become a water creature. You think we all live in the sea, and all your thoughts are devoted to sea life, fishes and other aquatic creatures. You forget that most of us live on land'.

Occasionally Clementine accompanied him but these were working voyages and not the sort of cruises she enjoyed. When visiting Malta and Gibraltar in May 1912, his party included the Prime Minister, Herbert Asquith. They sailed along the Italian coast but while Asquith and others went ashore visiting sites of antiquity, Churchill usually remained aboard.

Far left and right:
*Addressing munitions
workers in Enfield, famous
for the manufacture of Lee
Enfield rifles.*

Once, while on shore, Asquith complained that on his return he would be presented by Churchill with a long paper to read on oil. Asquith's daughter, Violet, noted in her diary, 'W incapable of lotus eating'. In describing the voyage she noted that Churchill 'hungered for the newspapers and pouches we should pick up at the next port of call whereas my father felt intense relief at their absence'.

Churchill's preoccupation with the Navy was insufficient to keep him from entering the fray when the subject of Ireland began to dominate British politics in 1911. The Conservatives together with their Unionist colleagues opposed the Irish Home Rule Bill, and the House of Lords, with their Conservative majority, rejected it. However, the Lords had power only to delay the bill, and, as it seemed destined eventually to become law, the opposition in Ulster mounted. Gun-running seemed

*Lieutenant-Colonel
Churchill with the officers of
the 6th Battalion Royal
Scots Fusiliers.*

to threaten civil war and Asquith was content for Churchill to assume increasing responsibility for Irish affairs. As usual he preached magnanimity from a position of strength. He advocated conciliation and compromise while the Royal Navy, with troops embarked, exercised in the Irish Sea. In mid-1914, when the outbreak of the First World War defused the crisis and united the nation, the Home Rule Bill was held in abeyance but Churchill's support for Home Rule was yet another issue which Conservatives would not forgive or forget.

The interlocking system of bilateral treaties then in existence between the major European powers led inevitably to world conflict when, on 28 June 1914, the heir to the Austrian throne was murdered by a Serbian assassin and in response Austria, allied to Germany, made unreasonable demands on Serbia whose guardian, Russia, was allied to France. Should Germany attack France, Belgium was the likely invasion route. Britain was inescapably involved in the unfolding events by her signature of 1839 to a treaty guaranteeing the independence and neutrality of Belgium. In Britain the Cabinet was divided, unwilling to see Britain engaged in a European war. Even Lloyd George seemed to waver. He was brought round, possibly by the bombardment of notes from Churchill across the Cabinet table.

In mid-July the British Fleet had coincidentally assembled for a review at Spithead and

was about to disperse when the European crisis deepened. On 28 July Austria refused to accept Serbia's response to their unreasonable ultimatum. Churchill cancelled the Fleet dispersal and by the end of the month the Fleet was at its war stations. On 2 August Germany declared war on Russia. On 3 August Germany declared war on France and invaded Belgium on 4 August. Germany had failed to reply to the British ultimatum demanding the maintenance of Belgium neutrality. By 11.00pm on 4 August Britain was also at war.

Churchill's hatred of war was born of his experience during the Boer War but now that hostilities had begun his policy was to prosecute it as vigorously as possible. He suggested a coalition government to remove the distraction of inter-party strife but Asquith preferred to stick with a Liberal Cabinet. In this Churchill was the one minister who understood war. The remainder were hopelessly at sea, giving Churchill an authoritative voice which was barely affected when Field Marshal Lord Kitchener, an experienced soldier but a political novice, joined as Secretary of State for War.

Demanding as it was, the war at sea did not fully occupy Churchill's attention. He made frequent visits to the Continent, having established naval armoured car squadrons and a naval air squadron in the vicinity of Dunkirk, He needed no encouragement when Kitchener and the Foreign Secretary, Sir Edward Grey, suggested he should rally the Belgians in Antwerp who were about to surrender the city to the Germans. He left within the hour, his train pulling out of Victoria Station at 1.30pm on the morning of 3 October. In his uniform of a cloak and yachting cap, he became the local Commander-in-Chief, dealt with the Belgian King and government and, often at considerable personal risk, rallied the defences. Antwerp held out for five more days, less than he had hoped for but enough to buy time for the British left flank to consolidate and hold Dunkirk.

Exhilarated by the experience, Churchill suggested handing over as First Lord and, providing a suitable military rank was granted him, continuing with a field command. Kitchener was prepared to make Churchill a Lieutenant-General but the Prime Minister needed Churchill at the Admiralty though he preferred to mask his need by making a joke of Churchill's suggestion. A seasoned general was sent out and the First Lord returned to learn that he had just become a father for the third time. Grey, writing to Clementine, praised her husband: 'I cannot tell you how much I admire his courage & gallant spirit & genius. It inspires us all'. In spite of his achievements there, Churchill's sally to Antwerp has often been cited in criticism of his judgement. At the time his critics suggested he had 'gone off his head'. Churchill himself later wrote that he should have remained in London

Herbert Kitchener (1850–1916)
1st Earl Kitchener of Khartoum

The most distinguished British military figure of his generation, Kitchener joined the Royal Engineers at the age of 21 and served in Palestine, Cyprus and the Sudan, where in 1898, as Commander-in-Chief of the Egyptian army, he was responsible for the final rout of the Muslim insurgents led by Mahdi.

The next phase of his career saw him as Chief-of-Staff and then Commander-in-Chief of the British forces in South Africa, which led to him being made a Viscount. Following positions as Commander-in-Chief in India and Pro-Consul-General in Egypt he received an Earldom. On the outbreak of war in 1914, he became Secretary of State for War in Asquith's government in which capacity he organised a massive recruiting campaign – the famous 'Your Country Needs You' posters bear his image. He died aboard the cruiser *Hampshire* when it was mined off the Orkney Islands while taking him to Russia.

Above: 'Plug Street', Lawrence Farm *by Winston Churchill, 1916. The painting, one of Churchill's first, shows the billet where he and other officers were housed.*

Right: *Trench periscope used by Churchill on the front line. He used the periscope from Clementine to lessen the risk of getting shot while surveying enemy positions, although usually he paid little attention to his own safety.*
He later gave the periscope to his adjutant, Captain Andrew Dewar Gibb.

Above right: *An army officer again. Churchill, seen here at Camblain l'Abbé near the Franco-Belgian border, served in the trenches in 1915–1916, firstly with the Grenadier Guards and then in command of the 6th Battalion, Royal Scots Fusiliers.*

Bottom right: *October 1918, in the Grande Place in Lille, the march past of the 47th Division celebrates the liberation of the city.*

and forced the Cabinet to take more effective action.

But the Cabinet was incapable of effective action. Churchill's authoritative voice did not reflect his actual authority, which did not extend beyond the Royal Navy. It was not until November that a War Council was formed. Consisting of senior ministers it was intended to formulate war policy but Asquith, a reluctant decision-maker at the best of times, had neither the knowledge nor the staff to help him decide between various options and coordinate action between departments. Churchill, searching for an alternative to the slaughter of trench warfare in France, devised a plan to attack through the Baltic, seizing the island of Borkum and linking up with the Russians. But no one else showed any enthusiasm for it. With the War Council bereft of leadership and meeting only once a week, the seeds of disaster were already germinating when, at the beginning of January 1915, Russia asked for British action against Germany's ally, Turkey.

With Russia under extreme pressure it was a request which could not be denied. It was agreed that the Dardanelles should be the point of attack and Churchill proposed a combined naval and military operation. Told by Kitchener that no troops could be spared, he decided, in spite of misgivings, that the navy should act alone. His decision was approved by the War Council and supported by Lord Fisher, brought back from retirement by Churchill to

Churchill as First Lord of the Admiralty.

become the First Sea Lord again. The plan was to force the Dardanelles, the narrow strait which led to the Sea of Marmara, and sail on to the Turkish capital, Constantinople. The prize was more than relief for Russia. If Turkey could be forced out of the war the allied armies could advance through the Balkans into the heart of Austria and the bloody stalemate in France would be broken.

In March 1915 the naval assault floundered in a minefield with the loss of four old battle-ships. Belatedly Kitchener found the troops which he had previously held back and respon-sibility for further operations passed into his hands. Churchill took no part in further

planning. The Turks, by now fully alerted to the situation, could not be dislodged by the Australian, British and New Zealand troops who landed at Gallipoli on 25 April and the campaign turned into yet another bloody battle of attrition which ended only when the last of the assaulting troops were withdrawn on 8 January 1916.

In May 1915 the capricious Lord Fisher had resigned. He had resigned before but on those occasions had been persuaded to stay. This time he had gone for good and the Conserv-ative opposition was now set to attack the government on its conduct of the war. None of the charges of lack of direction, indecision and prevarication could be laid at Churchill's door. His plans had been endorsed by the War Council and he was prepared to defend them in Parliament. Asquith, fearing political defeat, denied him this chance. Instead he invited the Conservatives to join the Liberals in government, the very solution Churchill had advocated at the outbreak of war. Ironically, the price the Conservatives exacted in joining a coalition was Churchill's dismissal from the Admiralty. They had achieved their revenge.

Nothing in his whole life left Churchill with such bitter feelings as the aftermath of the Dardanelles. He felt that a fraction of the resources which were being swallowed by the Western Front would have turned the whole course of the war if deployed as he had first wanted. Although Churchill remained a member of the Cabinet he no longer had any influence. 'I knew everything and could do nothing. I had great anxiety and no means of relieving it. I had to watch the unhappy casting away of great opportunities. And then it was the muse of painting came to my rescue'. It was a pastime from which he would derive great satisfaction and mental refreshment almost to the end of his long life. 'I know of nothing,' he wrote, 'which, without exhausting the body, more entirely occupies the mind'. However it could only occupy his mind from time to time and, frustrated that he was now no more than an observer of great events, he rejoined the army. In November 1915, at the age of 40, Churchill went to France as a major.

He spent a month with the 2nd Battalion, Grenadier Guards, accustoming himself to trench warfare. Twenty years earlier, after several close shaves on active service along the north-west frontier of India, he had written to his mother, 'I have faith in my star – that is that I am intended to do something in the world'. The guardian angel that watched over him in Cuba, India and during the Boer War was still in attendance. Moments after he had left his dugout a shell struck it, killing the man left behind.

In the New Year of 1916 Churchill took command of the 6th Battalion, Royal Scots Fusiliers. Badly knocked about at the recent battle of Loos, its depleted ranks filled with inexperienced recruits, its low morale became

even more depressed when it learned its new commanding officer was a discredited politician. But, from the accounts of officers and men who served under him, they were quickly won over. The battalion assistant adjutant, Lieutenant Jock McDavid, described how, 'After a very brief period he accelerated the morale of officers and men to an almost unbelievable degree. It was sheer personality. He let everyone under his command see that he was responsible, from the very moment he arrived, that they understood not only what they were supposed to do, by why they had to do it'. Churchill was unconventional. Nothing was too much trouble. Training was leavened with games and makeshift concerts. 'Poor fellows,' Churchill wrote to his wife, 'Nothing like this had ever been done for them before. They do not get much to brighten their lives – short though they may be'.

'War is a game to be played with a smiling face,' said Churchill to his officers as he led his battalion into the trenches near the village of Ploegsteert. He knew it was no game but when it had to be faced that was his philosophy. He accompanied patrols into no-man's-land, sharing dangers with junior officers and men. Lieutenant Hakewill Smith recalled, 'He never fell when a shell went off. He never ducked when a bullet went past with its loud crack. He used to say, after watching me duck, 'It's no damn use ducking; the bullet has gone a long way past you by now'.

But Churchill found that life in the front line was, for him, no escape from politics. He was concerned at the government's lack of drive. In particular he watched with dismay the pitiful progress in implementing the naval improvements he had instituted. When, in March, a parliamentary debate coincided with his leave from the front, he welcomed the chance to speak. He put forward a skilful and reasoned criticism of Admiralty policy which began to raise serious misgivings among his listeners until he proposed a remedy: the return of Lord Fisher to invigorate the faltering programmes. But Fisher was not remembered for his undoubted energy, only for his irrational behaviour during the Dardanelles campaign. Thus, Balfour, who had become First Lord on Churchill's dismissal, had only to pour ridicule on the proposal to deflect the valid criticisms of his naval policies.

Churchill had failed to judge parliamentary opinion. His words, prompted by anguish at the apathy in high places, had been taken as a naive attempt at his own reinstatement. When Margot Asquith, the Prime Minister's wife, wrote that Churchill was 'a fool of the lowest judgement and contemptible,' she was reflecting a large segment of parliamentary opinion. A few voices knew that Churchill's criticisms, if not his remedy, were well founded. Lord Esher, a permanent member of the Imperial Committee of Defence, was aware that 'Churchill's outburst was the culmination

of a great deal of discontent in the Fleet itself'. But this was no comfort to Churchill, who once more turned his back on his enemies at home and crossed the Channel to face the ones in France.

From the moment he began to paint, easel and paint-box accompanied Churchill wherever he went. His earliest paintings include ruined buildings and exploding shells at Ploegsteert. He set up his easel in the courtyard of the farm which served as his headquarters and painted even as shells exploded round about. Hakewill Smith recalled Churchill saying, 'I couldn't get that shell hole right. However I did it, it looked like a mountain, but yesterday I discovered that if I put a bit of white in it, it looked like a hole after all'.

In spite of his recent parliamentary humiliation Churchill felt he would do more good back in politics than commanding a battalion in France, and it is likely he would have returned in March 1916 but for Clementine's wise counsel. On the one hand she worried over his safety, 'If I say stay where you are a wicked bullet may find you'. On the other hand she judged that a precipitate return would be misunderstood politically. She showed her sure political touch when she wrote, 'To be great one's actions must be understood by simple people. Your motive for going to the Front was easy to understand. Your motive for coming back requires explanation. That was why your Fisher speech was not a success – people could not understand it'. So for the moment Churchill remained a soldier.

A motive for returning presented itself in May when the 6th and 7th Royal Scots Fusiliers were amalgamated under the command of the colonel of the 7th, he being a regular officer. There was no immediate prospect of a further command for Churchill and he arrived back in London at the end of the first week in May. He had as much political experience as any of the Cabinet and a great deal more knowledge of war, yet he remained cast aside. Lloyd George was his one ally. He spoke frequently in Parliament and was almost as frequently interrupted by the cry, 'What about the Dardanelles?' Asquith resolutely refused to make public any documents which would have exonerated Churchill while Kitchener, who might have been forced to admit a large portion of responsibility for the debacle, had been drowned when the warship on which he was travelling hit a mine.

The lack-lustre government of Asquith fell in December 1916 and Churchill had high hopes of a Cabinet appointment when Lloyd George became Prime Minister. In late May and June 1917 he undertook, with the Prime Minister's approval, a visit to the French and British Fronts but it was not until July that Lloyd George felt able to disregard Conservative hostility to Churchill and appoint him Minister of Munitions. He immediately settled long-running industrial disputes which were threat-

ening production and established munitions factories behind the lines in France to shorten the logistic chain. His talents as a roving emissary were fully employed by Lloyd George and he established an office at the Chateau Vechrocq, near St Omer, enabling him to stay in France for days at a time.

The First World War ended on 11 November 1918. An election a month later saw Lloyd George returned as the head of a continuing coalition government. In this Churchill became Secretary of State for War and Air with the huge administrative task of demobilising well over two million men while simultaneously organising a further million men in the army of occupation in Germany and the garrisons in

As Colonial Secretary after the war, Churchill set up and chaired the Cairo Conference to settle the future of large parts of Arabia. T E Lawrence ('Lawrence of Arabia') is fourth from the right in the second row.

At Epping during the 1924
General Election campaign.
Elected just before his 50th
birthday, Churchill would
represent this constituency
for 40 years, retiring only
months before his death.

Stanley Baldwin

1st Earl Baldwin of Bewdley

Baldwin's legacy is disputed, being remembered largely for his appeasement of Nazi Germany in the 1930s. However, some would argue that his domestic policies, although resulting in Britain being insufficiently armed, at least left it united when war came.

An ironmaster's son, born in 1867, Stanley Baldwin went into the family manufacturing business after education at Harrow and Cambridge. He did not enter the House of Commons until he was forty-one when he took over his deceased father's Conservative seat. The turning point in his political career came when he was appointed President of the Board of Trade in 1921. A year later, when the Conservatives returned to power, he became Chancellor of the Exchequer.

On the retirement in 1923 of Andrew Bonar Law through ill health, Baldwin became Prime Minister. Within eight months his government was defeated on a motion of confidence and for ten months he led the opposition against a Labour administration. With the Conservatives back in office Baldwin remained Prime Minister until 1929, a period which saw the General Strike of 1926. In 1931 he became Lord President of the Council when the Conservative Party entered into a coalition with the Labour Prime Minister, Ramsay MacDonald. MacDonald retired in 1935 and Baldwin again became Prime Minister.

Accused by Churchill in 1936 of neglecting Britain's defences he replied that he could think of nothing more likely to lose an election than seeking a mandate to rearm. Putting electoral success before national safety was to Churchill 'an incident without parallel in our Parliamentary history.' Baldwin stands condemned by his own frankness but there is little doubt that a call to rearm would have resulted in an electoral defeat, especially with memories of the First World War still fresh in the public mind, and it seems unlikely that any government could have implemented a policy of rearmament.

In 1936 Baldwin surmounted the political problems surrounding the Abdication. Following the coronation of King George VI in 1937, he retired. He died in 1947.

Palestine, Mesopotamia and India. Field Marshal Sir Douglas Haig, the British Commander-in-Chief, remarked in his diary on Churchill's courage, foresight and statesmanship: 'All of these qualities most of his colleagues seem to have lacked throughout this war'.

These qualities, apart from being deployed to implement the huge demobilisation scheme, were soon put to the test in Russia where British forces, sent there by Churchill's predecessors, were co-operating with the anti-Bolshevik forces. If the Bolsheviks succeeded, Churchill saw 'a plague bearing' Russia which would menace the world. The disease needed stamping out before it could spread. But Britain, unlike its ebullient Secretary of State for War and Air, was more war-weary than he supposed. His attempts to ship war materials to aid the Poles in their war against Bolshevik Russia in 1920 were frustrated by Ernest Bevin, a trades union leader who, in 1940, would become a leading member of Churchill's government.

The cabinet were lukewarm. 'If Russia is to be saved,' said Lloyd George, ' it must be saved by Russians'. Churchill argued that, far from Britain fighting the battles of the anti-Bolsheviks, they were 'fighting ours', a fact which became apparent only many years later. However, Churchill greatly underestimated the scale of the task and his Russian venture failed. Britain had not the resources to alter the out-

A University Man

Churchill took a keen interest in education and this picture shows him taking part in a Belfast University Rag Week procession in 1926. He became Chancellor of the University of Bristol in 1929, holding the position until his death and was a stalwart supporter of the university and the city. In 1941, having watched German bombers attack Bristol docks the night before, he presented honorary degrees to the Australian Prime Minister, Robert Menzies, and the American Ambassador, John Winant. His daughter, Mary recalled the people arriving for the ceremony with their ceremonial robes over their fire-fighting clothes, which were still wet.

In accordance with his wishes, Churchill College, Cambridge, was founded in 1959. Churchill decreed its goal was 'to offer an education as high as any that exists to meet the challenge of the new age of technology'.

Displaying his customary humour on receiving an honorary degree at the University of Miami he said, 'No one ever passed so many examinations and received so many degrees'.

come, and although Churchill's sentiments were right, the accusation of running a private war in Russia was one more charge his political enemies would resurrect from time to time and the one they would use when pinning on him the label of warmonger.

By the end of the First World War the British army was occupying large areas of what had been the Turkish Empire. These included Palestine and Mesopotamia (now Iraq), both of which were to be mandated to Britain by the League of Nations, a mandate which endorsed the Balfour Declaration of 1917 under which a national home for the Jews was to be estab-lished in Palestine. Churchill, responsible for maintaining these armies of occupation and frustrated by other departments with fingers in the pie, suggested setting up a Middle East Department to concentrate the existing divided interests within a single department. The Colonial Secretary, Lord Milner, could see the problems ahead and declared he would have nothing to do with these increased and heavy responsibilities. Not surprisingly Churchill was appointed in his place and within the month had arrived in Cairo to settle the whole compli-cated problem of the Middle East in which Arab hostility towards the Balfour Declaration played a large part.

The conference opened on 12 March 1921. All the decisions arrived at would still need to be agreed by the British Cabinet and ratified by a vote in Parliament, so there were many opinions for Churchill to take into account. Not the least of his difficulties was the balance of opinion in Britain where nine-tenths of the establishment supported the Arabs rather than the Jews.

Mesopotamia took up the first five days during which a new kingdom was established and King Feisal placed on the throne. On the sixth day the conference turned to Palestine which Churchill had decided would be sepa-rated from Transjordan where Feisal's brother, Abdullah, was already lined up to become the ruler. Their father, King Hussein, in the adjacent Hedajz, and Ibn Saud, ruler of the

rest of Arabia, would receive subsidies from
Britain. If Abdullah was won over, many influential Arabs were not. In Jerusalem Churchill
was presented with a protest declaring the
Balfour Declaration a 'gross injustice'. He
replied robustly, concluding, 'If instead of
sharing miseries through quarrels you will
share blessings through co-operation, a bright
and tranquil future lies before your country'.

In attempting to reconcile Jewish and Arab
interests Churchill seems to have got the
balance right as the settlement provoked
protests in equal measure from both sides.
Churchill returned to London in mid-April but
it was not until June that he was called upon to
defend his policies in Parliament when his
statement swung the establishment behind
him. The Prime Minister thought Churchill's
performance one of his 'very best' while other
senior politicians, some of whom regarded him
with envy and others as a loose cannon, also
applauded him.

At the end of June Lady Randolph died.
Churchill was saddened but this did not inhibit
his constant flow of ideas across the entire
business of government. On 4 July at a conference of Dominion Prime Ministers he spoke
against renewing the Anglo-Japanese Alliance
of 1902, advocating instead an alliance with
America. The Foreign Secretary, Lord Curzon,
was furious that the Colonial Secretary should
intervene in a Foreign Office matter. Others
took Curzon's side, including Lloyd George

Perhaps as a reaction against his own childhood, Churchill was a caring and affectionate father. He is seen here at Chartwell with his youngest daughter Mary, shortly after they moved there in 1924.

who wrote, 'I have done my best to stopper his fizzing'. Churchill was unrepentant, writing to Curzon, 'In these great matters we must be allowed to have opinions'. He also went against the grain of the conference when, seeking reconciliation in Europe, he suggested the British Empire should be 'the ally of France and the friend of Germany'.

By now the political intimacy between Churchill and Lloyd George was waning.

Churchill had taken the lead in Cabinet in pressing for imaginative measures to combat unemployment and foster a more egalitarian social policy. But the Prime Minister had made no plans to absorb into the workforce the huge numbers of demobilised soldiers who Churchill feared were likely to turn to the Labour Party at the next election. The two men had different views of the Bolshevik menace and Lloyd George had wearied of the constant arguments. Lloyd George once compared Churchill to a chauffeur who after months of sane and skilful driving suddenly took you over the precipice.

The Prime Minister was undoubtedly speaking for the majority of the Cabinet when he reminded Churchill that it was not possible to hold a conversation with someone bent on delivering a monologue. Churchill was undoubtedly a difficult colleague. Field Marshal Sir Henry Wilson noted that while many of his good qualities were hidden all of his bad ones were 'in the shop window'. The fact was that the loquacious Churchill, ambitious for ever more responsibility, could never be confined to a single department and forever sought wider fields. It was not a matter of power for power's sake but, as he had said to his constituents at Dundee 12 years earlier, 'to make this muddled world a better place'. But Lloyd George was too canny a politician to allow a potential rival that much scope.

The political tension between the two men did not deter Lloyd George from using

Below: *Bricklaying with his daughter Sarah at Chartwell, 1928. The brick wall which still stands around the kitchen garden was built largely by Churchill's own hands.*

Bottom: *With Randolph at the start of a boar hunt near Dieppe, 1928.*

Churchill as a conciliator between the British government and Sinn Fein leaders whose terrorist tactics were threatening the rule of law in Ireland. Churchill had been an advocate of the Irish Home Rule Bill before the war but subsequently, as Secretary of State for War in 1920, had supported a policy of repression when Sinn Fein turned to terror. He had deployed a counter-insurgency force, the 'Black and Tans', as they became known because of the colour of their uniform, which met terrorism with terror. When the situation continued to deteriorate and Lloyd George called a truce on 11 July 1921, Churchill, as Colonial Secretary, had been settling the Middle East but, having watched events in Ireland, was in the mood to mediate. He was only one of a delegation of seven which included Lloyd George but there is no doubt that the rapport he struck with Michael Collins, the Sinn Fein leader, was crucial to the signing of the Irish Treaty in December 1921. Subsequently he was the midwife at the some-what difficult birth of the Irish Provisional Government.

In 1922 Turkish forces, driving the Greeks before them in a campaign to regain what had been Turkish territory, came up against the British garrison at Chanak on the Dardanelles. Lloyd George appointed Churchill the chairman of a Cabinet committee to oversee the British military reaction. The garrison was reinforced and after a tense stand-off the situ-

ation was resolved without a shot being fired
but it provided those Conservatives, who had
become restive in the Coalition Government, to
withdraw their co-operation. At this moment
Churchill was being operated on for appen-
dicitis, then a far more serious operation than
now, and he was recovering in a nursing home
when Lloyd George resigned on 19 October
and the Conservatives formed a government.

Still recovering from his operation, Churchill
was too ill to campaign in the election which
was called for November. When Clementine
took his place on the hustings she met political
hostility and personal abuse in his predominantly working class constituency of Dundee.
She portrayed him as the peacemaker he was
at heart, but the Dundee newspapers and the
proletarian voters, recalling his anti-Bolshevik
policies, saw him only as a warmonger.
Churchill travelled to Dundee a week before

the voting. Still with the stitches from his
operation he was too weak to perform with his
usual vigour and on one occasion was forced to
abandon his speech in face of what the *Dundee
Courier* described as 'a howling mob'.

The poll put the Conservatives back in office
after an interval of 17 years. At Dundee
Churchill came fourth leaving him, as he put it,
'without an office, without a seat, without a
party and without an appendix'. His friends
commiserated but Churchill, alive to the
changing political map, replied to one friend,
'If you saw the kind of lives the Dundee folk
have to live, you would admit they have many
excuses'. He saw that socialism, which he
abhorred, would spread, and understood the
reasons. He also saw that the Liberals, over-
taken numerically by the Labour Party, could
no longer effectively oppose it.

Churchill, never a typical party politician,
had long toyed with the idea of a centre party
and speaking earlier in the year had put the
case for a new National Party made up of both
Conservatives and Liberals and free from the
tensions in a coalition government. As a
Liberal he had been a centre-left Home Secretary but the Russian venture and the emer-
gence of the Labour Party had moved him to
the right. He was edging back towards the
Conservatives although essentially he would
always remain a man of the centre. He was in
no hurry to decide his place in the shifting
political scene and two days after his forty-

eighth birthday moved with his family to the South of France where he had rented a villa near Cannes to paint and continue work on his history of the war, entitled *The World Crisis*.

Before leaving he had bought Chartwell Manor, in Kent. In the years to come he would personally lay the bricks for the walls of a cottage and the kitchen garden, landscape the grounds and create ponds, dams and lakes. To him it was stability. To Clementine it was a financial worry for, in spite of his lucrative literary and journalistic ventures, they would always suffer from rickety finances until 1946, when a collection of friends bought Chartwell and presented it to the nation on the condition that the Churchills remained in residence for their lifetimes.

The first volume of *The World Crisis* was published two months later to laudatory reviews. 'A whale among minnows' wrote the *Observer*. The *New Statesman* thought it 'egotistical but honest'. In dealing with events when he was First Lord of the Admiralty it is not surprising that he justified his policies, but he was also self-critical admitting, 'I seem to have been too ready to undertake tasks which were hazardous or even forlorn'. Balfour, the butt of Churchill's criticism in 1916, was no doubt getting his own back when he observed that Winston had written a 'big book about himself and called it *The World Crisis*'. The sarcastic wit was wide of the mark for although Churchill wrote of events in which he had been

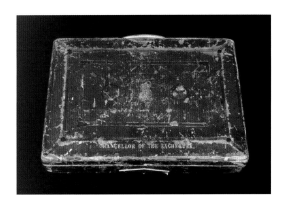

Churchill's cane and top hat: The cane was given to him as a wedding present by King Edward VII, in 1908.

Below: *Every Chancellor of the Exchequer carried his budget plans to Parlliament in this box. Know as the 'Gladstone box', it was used by successive Chancellors, including Churchill, from the 1860s to 1997.*

personally involved, he covered the entire war on all fronts, on land and at sea, in great detail. His analysis of such epic battles as Jutland and the Somme is masterly. *The World Crisis* ran to six volumes, published between 1923 and 1931.

Where his knowledge was limited, Churchill enlisted expert help. In the scientific field he turned to Professor Frederick Lindemann whom he met in 1921 and who would remain his scientific adviser for another 30 years.

Returning from France after six months
Churchill began to consider how war would be
shaped by scientific developments. He was 20
years ahead of his time when he wrote 'Might
not a bomb no bigger than an orange be found
to possess a secret power to concentrate the
power of a 1000 tons of cordite and blast a
township at a stroke? Could not explosives
even of the existing type be guided automati-
cally in flying machines without a pilot, in
ceaseless procession upon a hostile city?'

The Liberals would have found Churchill a
safe seat in Parliament but he had abandoned
them. In January 1924 the Conservatives were
defeated in Parliament and Stanley Baldwin
who had taken over as Prime Minister from
Bonar Law, resigned. Ramsay MacDonald
became Prime Minister of a Labour government dependent on Liberal support. Angered at
Labour's economic assistance to Bolshevik
Russia, Churchill was anxious to return to
Parliament where his influence would be more
directly felt than through public speeches and
articles in the press. In a by-election in March
he stood unsuccessfully as an Independent and
remained without hope of a satisfactory seat
until courted by Stanley Baldwin who,
preferring to have a political heavyweight
within his tent than outside, offered him the
safe Conservative seat of Epping. At a General
Election in October 1924 the Conservatives
were returned to power and Baldwin appointed
him Chancellor of the Exchequer. In November

Churchill celebrated his 50th birthday and
announced his return to the Conservative
Party.

Churchill's first significant job as Chancellor
was to represent Britain at a conference in
Paris to settle all war debts. In the space of a
week he had negotiated a deal by which
Britain's debt payments to America would be
accompanied by payments to Britain by all her
principal debtors. Britain became the better off
by £1,000 million pounds.

As Chancellor of the Exchequer Churchill
introduced five budgets between 1924 and
1929. Budget day in April was a fixed event in
the parliamentary year and Churchill had only
a few months to master the details of what
would be the most significant of his budgets.
He had arrived as Chancellor with no strategy
mapped out, few ideas of fiscal management
and no great interest in economic theory. The
Treasury officials, on the other hand, were
naturally well versed in all the details, had a
ready-made plan for which, they said, the time
was right. Their plan, supported by the Bank of
England, was to return Britain to the pre-war
Gold Standard in order to recover for the City
of London the financial supremacy it had
enjoyed when international currencies were
pegged to a fixed rate of exchange expressed
in their value in gold.

It was generally conceded that the return to
the Gold Standard was a technical matter for
the experts at the Treasury and Bank but, true

to form, Churchill did not accept expert advice without question. He took a broader view than his officials, being more concerned with social reform, the economic divide between North and South, unemployment and the lack of understanding between the City and industry. He would rather see 'finance less proud and industry more content'. To his Treasury mandarin he wrote: 'The Governor of the Bank of England shows himself perfectly happy in the spectacle of Britain possessing the finest credit in the world simultaneously with a million and quarter unemployed'. After reviewing other factors the letter concluded, 'The fact that this island with its enormous extraneous resources is unable to maintain its population is surely a cause for the deepest heart-searching. Forgive me for adding to your labours by these Sunday morning reflections'.

The Prime Minister, a former Chancellor, was in favour of returning to the Gold Standard and eventually, having canvassed widely, Churchill fell in with his officials and Britain returned to the old system. The press and the establishment approved the decision. Churchill later told his doctor that it was the worst decision he had made in his life. In time the press and the establishment would agree. But politically, in 1925, it was inevitable: the Conservative Party would otherwise have been furious.

Although the return to the Gold Standard is the feature most frequently criticised and

focussed upon, Churchill's first budget was more noteworthy for its social content, notably pensions for all at 65 and for widows and orphans from the moment of their bereavement. Income tax was reduced for the lowest income groups. Speaking a fortnight later to the British Bankers' Association, Churchill emphasised the need for 'national policy' and 'the appeasement of class bitterness'. His four subsequent Budgets reflected these sentiments but were less sensational than the first. Conservatives disliked his liberal tendencies and forced him to moderate some of his plans.

In 1926 the Trades Union Congress called a General Strike in support of the miners who, when they demanded an increase in wages, were locked out by the mine owners. Churchill had originally been inclined to side with 'our much abused coal miners' and when a nation-wide strike threatened spoke in conciliatory terms. However, the moment workers downed tools he became more robust; the strikers needed to be taught that they could not take on the State. Baldwin preferred a softer line, appreciating that many were unhappy to have become involved and foreseeing that the strike would crumble. Churchill produced the *British Gazette* which, with a circulation which reached over a quarter of a million, dissemi-nated news in the absence of the national press. Churchill wrote much of the copy himself and submitted unwillingly when the Cabinet demanded a softening of its tone.

Not surprisingly the Chancellor who had recently done so much for their families did not endear himself to the workers. But, when the strike crumbled after nine days, Churchill became once more the benevolent paternalist whom Baldwin left in charge of negotiations while he took his annual holiday in France. The General Strike was over but the miners remained out. Churchill attempted throughout the summer to resolve the dispute, seeking a national minimum wage and suggesting a tribunal to adjudicate. The Cabinet rejected both measures and, with the Government unwilling to interfere, it was left to the two sides to fight to a conclusion in November.

Churchill was 52. In January 1927 in Malta he played his last game of polo before travelling through Italy where he met Mussolini to the anger of Liberals and Labour at home. This was followed by a holiday in France where he continued working on *The World Crisis* and corresponding on a variety of subjects to his Cabinet colleagues. In 1929 he presented his fifth and final budget with a speech lasting almost three hours which, in the words of Neville Chamberlain, 'kept the House fascinated by its wit, audacity, adroitness and power'.

Two weeks later, a General Election having been called, Churchill made his first radio broadcast urging his listeners to 'avoid three-card trick men and above all avoid, as you would the smallpox, class warfare and violent political strife'. Churchill was re-elected but class warfare was rife and Ramsay MacDonald's Labour Party were swept into office for the second time.

A rare moment of leisure in the study at Chartwell.

3

WILDERNESS TO WAR 1929–40

In 1939 Churchill worked at home at Chartwell on his four-volume History of The English Speaking Peoples.

Out of office, Churchill left Britain at the beginning of August 1929 for a three-month tour of Canada and the United States. Writing in advance to an American friend, Bernard Baruch, he declared, 'I want to see the country and meet the leaders of its fortunes'. To the foremost American newspaper proprietor, William Randolph Hearst, he wrote, 'We must discuss the future of the world even if we cannot decide it'.

After speaking engagements in Canada's major cities, Churchill travelled south from Vancouver through the United States to Hollywood before turning east and returning to Chicago and New York. The theme of his speeches throughout the North American continent was the need for Anglo-American co-operation. It was not a subject to which most Americans were giving much thought, but the British Consul-General in San Francisco noted 'the wonderful and immediate results' of Churchill's visit. His discussions with Hearst resulted in more lucrative newspaper articles. In Hollywood, he made friends with Charlie Chaplin whom he described as 'Bolshy in politics and delightful in conversation'.

The collapse of the stock market occurred

when Churchill was in New York, an event which affected him personally for, having invested much of his literary earnings there, he lost some quarter of a million pounds in today's money. Characteristically he took the long view, 'This financial disaster, cruel as it is to thousands, is only a passing episode in the march of a valiant and serviceable people'. For Churchill it meant writing more frantically than ever to maintain his life-style.

Churchill returned to London in time to hear that the Conservatives were to support the Labour government's plans to fulfil Lloyd George's wartime promise to grant India dominion status, ie near-independence within the British Empire, like Canada and Australia had. Churchill considered that India was nowhere near ready for such a measure, advocating instead provincial autonomy under a central government firmly in British hands. He warned that the proposed policy would lead to civil unrest between Hindu and Moslem. The Untouchables, the lowest caste, 'denied by the Hindu religion even the semblance of human rights', would no longer have a guardian.

The Indian political leader, Jawaharlal Nehru, demanded full independence and

Churchill held his seat in the General Election of 1929, but the Conservatives lost power to Ramsay MacDonald's Labour Party. No longer Chancellor of the Exchequer, he embarked on a tour of North America that included a number of speaking engagements, meetings with the famous and influential, and a successful fishing trip in California during which he landed this 188lb marlin.

launched a campaign of civil disobedience to British rule. Mahatma Gandhi, a British-educated barrister turned Indian spiritual leader, added his weight to this but called off the campaign after being invited to a series of talks with the Viceroy, Lord Irwin. 'A seditious Middle Temple lawyer, now posing as a fakir of a type well-known in the East, striding half naked up the steps of the Viceregal Palace,' was Churchill's characteristic comment on the event.

A speech in Parliament by Churchill in January 1930, criticising the Conservative Indian policy, marked a definite break with party leaders and led to Churchill resigning from the Opposition front bench. Churchill had the support of some 60 MPs who felt they had not been sufficiently consulted on the matter but, in the face of the parliamentary alliance between MacDonald and Baldwin, was unable to influence the outcome.

In mid-1931 the second Labour government ran out of steam, defeated by economic difficulties. The National Government which was then formed of all parties under Ramsay MacDonald went to the polls on 27 October and received overwhelming endorsement. Churchill, who was returned with a hugely increased majority, remained isolated on the backbenches.

When, in December, Parliament debated the need to continue moving India towards dominion status, only 43 voted with Churchill while 369 voted with the government. Undoubtedly Churchill's reputation suffered seriously from his strident opposition to the general consensus on India. By the time the India Bill was passed in 1935, Churchill was past 60, still always interesting but only a marginal figure in politics. Thus, for too long, his warnings fell on deaf ears when he tried to draw attention to the growing threat from Hitler and a resurgent Germany.

Meanwhile in December 1931, together with Clementine and their daughter Diana, Churchill set off for the United States, determined to recoup his losses in the crash of 1929. He had contracted to give 40 lectures and to write a series of articles for the *Daily Mail*. Two days after his arrival, having given only one lecture, he was knocked down by a car and seriously injured. His telegraphed account of the accident to the *Daily Mail* was syndicated worldwide, his article bringing thousands of telegrams and letters wishing him a quick recovery. His political influence in Parliament may have waned but his profile was as prominent as ever. After a rest in the Bahamas he returned to New York and in three weeks lectured in 19 cities, earning £7,500, half as much again as a Cabinet Minister's annual salary.

Other sources of much-needed income were also now coming on stream. *My Early Life*, an autobiography taking readers as far as September 1908 'when I married and lived happily ever after', had been published in 1930

and was selling well, eventually being translated into 13 languages. His journalism was as prolific as ever and he had started on *Marlborough: His Life and Times*, which had brought in a good advance. *Marlborough* would be published in four volumes of which the first appeared in 1933. The work had a contemporary resonance for the author's attitude to the events then unfolding in Europe reflecting his study of his great ancestor's successful European campaigns during the 17th century and the political alliances which made them possible.

By now Churchill was expressing concern both at the increasing influence of Hitler in

On tour in America with (left to right) his son Randolph, his nephew Johnny and brother Jack.

Château St Georges Motel,
c.1930.

The Loup River, Alpes Martines, 1936.

Germany and the call from Britain for general disarmament. He had not been in a position to moderate the 'malignant and futile' Allied demands imposed upon Germany under the Treaty of Versailles and saw the dangers of disarming in a situation where smouldering German grievances might be fanned into flames. Unlike most people in Britain, Churchill understood Hitler's aggressive intentions from the beginning and, whereas the government saw disarmament as the road to peace, Churchill saw military strength as the bulwark against war. His call to negotiate from a position of strength was a policy he would continue to advocate but MacDonald and Baldwin, in their pursuit of general disarmament, went so far as to set an example by reducing the strength of the Royal Air Force.

In January 1933 Hitler became Chancellor of Germany. Within a few weeks several thousand opponents of Nazism had been arrested and popular demands aired in Germany for German rearmament. Churchill was not content to argue only from a gut feeling; he developed his own sources of information which in most cases were superior to those of the government, or at least to those that the government released publicly. Major Desmond Morton, who headed the Industrial Intelligence Centre (1929–1939), Squadron Leader Torr Anderson of the Royal Air Force and Ralph Wigram from the Foreign Office, all concerned with the deficiencies in Britain's

Far left: *Campaigning in Epping in 1929.*

Right: *Entertaining family and friends at Chartwell, 1931. Left to right: Tom Mitford (Clementine's cousin and brother of the famous Mitford sisters), Freddie Birkenhead (son of the distinguished lawyer and Conservative politician, F E Smith), Winston, Clementine, Diana, Randolph and Charlie Chaplin.*

defences, provided him with information at some risk to themselves. From Sir Henry Strakosch, a banker and industrialist, came reliable figures on German rearmament. As Churchill's arguments began to tell, other sources came forward until, in March 1935, the government admitted serious deficiencies in the three Services and belatedly increased defence expenditure.

In mid-1935, MacDonald was unable through illness to continue in office and Baldwin became Prime Minister. Churchill hoped that his breach with Baldwin was over and that he would be included in the government but was disappointed to find himself still out in the cold. Baldwin was grooming Neville Chamberlain to succeed as Prime Minister and the last thing he wanted was to see Churchill in a position where he would become the front-runner.

In 1936 Hitler marched into the Rhineland, the German territory along the French border which had been demilitarised at the end of the war. To Baldwin, set on appeasement, this was simply Hitler moving into 'his own backyard'. To Churchill, Hitler's action, and Britain and France's reaction to it, was more a matter of 'funk versus honour'. Speaking in Parliament a month later Churchill thought that Austria would be next on the list and asked in vain for Britain to take the initiative in forming an 'effective union' of the countries which seemed to be threatened. On holiday in France he visited the Maginot Line defences – holidays were always working holidays, much of them spent writing, painting being about the only true holiday pursuit.

Churchill's position was strengthening by the day. Serving officers, alarmed at Britain's parlous defences, were turning to him. Many Members of Parliament felt that the Prime Minister and his Cabinet had no grip of a worsening situation. The Labour leader, Clement Attlee, sent a private message that he would support any rearmament programme Churchill proposed. Then in December 1936 came an extraordinary misjudgement which shattered in an instant the support he had patiently built up in Parliament during the preceding two years.

The Prince of Wales had succeeded his father as King Edward VIII in January 1936. His name was linked with Wallis Simpson who was about to divorce her second husband. Churchill, who had been friends with the new King for many years did not approve of his choice and began to work behind the scenes to persuade Mrs Simpson to abandon the idea of marriage to the King. A crisis arose when the King informed Baldwin of the situation. Baldwin's response was that the King should choose between the throne or Mrs Simpson, to which the King replied that if so it would have to be Mrs Simpson.

With Baldwin's concurrence Churchill tried to persuade him not to abdicate so hastily. The King had already made up his mind to marry Mrs Simpson, but misled Churchill by asking for more time. Having reported to Baldwin and confident that more time would be allowed, Churchill reassured the King on this point. He went further, drafting a statement for the King to declare that he would not enter into a marriage contrary to the advice of his ministers. Thinking that the King would accept this Churchill asked Parliament 'that no irrevo-cable step will be taken before the House has received a full statement'. To his surprise there were immediate cries of derision which prevented his explanation that he was simply attempting to avoid a constitutional crisis by providing more time. The King abdicated and the majority of MPs took the view that Churchill had been attempting to lead a revolt

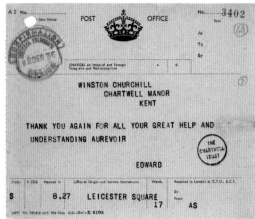

against Baldwin. The press and public once again branded him a wayward genius with suspect judgement.

At the end of May 1937 Baldwin retired and Chamberlain became Prime Minister. Throughout 1937 and 1938 Churchill's sources of information continued to grow and his warnings grew ever more urgent. However, Chamberlain was even more of an appeaser than his predecessor. He was mainly concerned with improving relations with Germany and not with relative military strengths. It is true that Britain had begun to rearm but without real conviction and against the background of several lost years.

In March 1938 Germany annexed Austria. Churchill, concerned that Czechoslovakia would be Hitler's next victim, advocated an arrangement of collective defence for the small states of Europe who, he said, had to be

Adolf Hitler (1889–1945)

Apart from his decoration for bravery during the First World War Hitler was a failure for the first half of his life. However, by claiming that the post-war treaties were intended to keep Germany in a subservient position, he was able to play upon the emotions of all sections of the population and in 1933 became Chancellor, beginning to realise his vision of a German Reich dominating Europe. Jews were outlawed and the swastika became the national flag. Adjacent territories were annexed under the pretext of giving people *Liebensraum* (living space). His invasion of Poland in 1939 led directly to the outbreak of the Second World War. At first the war went well for Germany, but from the end of 1941 the tide turned. Key factors such as Britain's refusal to submit even when standing alone, Hitler's attack on Russia and his retreat following German defeat at Stalingrad, US entry into the war, Montgomery's victory over Rommel at El Alamein and the Allied invasion of Normandy made the outcome inevitable. With the Russians on the point of capturing Berlin, Hitler committed suicide on 30 April 1945.

encouraged to feel they could rely on Britain. He pressed the government to associate itself with a French declaration to support Czechoslovakia if she became the victim of unprovoked aggression. But, with Germany threatening Czechoslovakia and Britain lagging in military terms, Chamberlain judged that appeasement was the only choice for Britain. A joint declaration with France might have been a viable option but Chamberlain preferred appeasement, hoping that war would be averted if Czechoslovakia accepted the loss of the Sudetenland, the areas of Czechoslovakia bordering Germany.

At his own invitation, Chamberlain flew to Germany three times in a fortnight. He agreed, together with France, that Hitler could annex the Sudetenland. Returning on 30 September 1938 he waved a piece of paper carrying Hitler's signature, which he said, was a guarantee 'of peace for our time.' The sense of relief which swept the country was accompanied by some unease. Speaking in Parliament Churchill declared, 'we have suffered a total and unmitigated defeat'. He did not grudge the people their 'natural, spontaneous outburst of joy and relief when they learned that the hard ordeal would no longer be required of them at the moment; but they should know the truth'. Britain had 'sustained a defeat without a war'. The Western democracies had been 'weighed in the balance and found wanting'. He concluded, 'and do not suppose that this is the

end. This is only the beginning of the reckoning. This is only the first sip, the first foretaste of the bitter cup which will be proffered to us year by year unless by a supreme recovery of moral health and martial vigour, we rise again and take our stand for freedom as in the olden time.'

In March 1939 Hitler marched into the rest of Czechoslovakia and began to apply pressure on Poland, specifically for the Polish Corridor and the Free City of Danzig to return to the Reich. Chamberlain now gave a guarantee to Poland which, as Churchill pointed out in Parliament, was a guarantee of independence but not the integrity of its borders. Churchill rightly saw that, if it appeased Hitler, Chamberlain would let Danzig fall as he had the Sudetenland. In July large posters asking 'What Price Churchill?' appeared in the Strand and Piccadilly Circus and there was a general clamour for him to be included in the government. Chamberlain still resisted, writing to his sister, 'If Winston got into the Government it would not be long before we would be at war'.

In fact war was already on the doorstep. In late August Germany strengthened her position by a non-aggression pact with Russia, at which Britain signed a treaty of alliance with Poland. Hitler hesitated for six days and on 1 September invaded Poland. Still Chamberlain prevaricated, sending a final ultimatum to Hitler two days later. When this was ignored

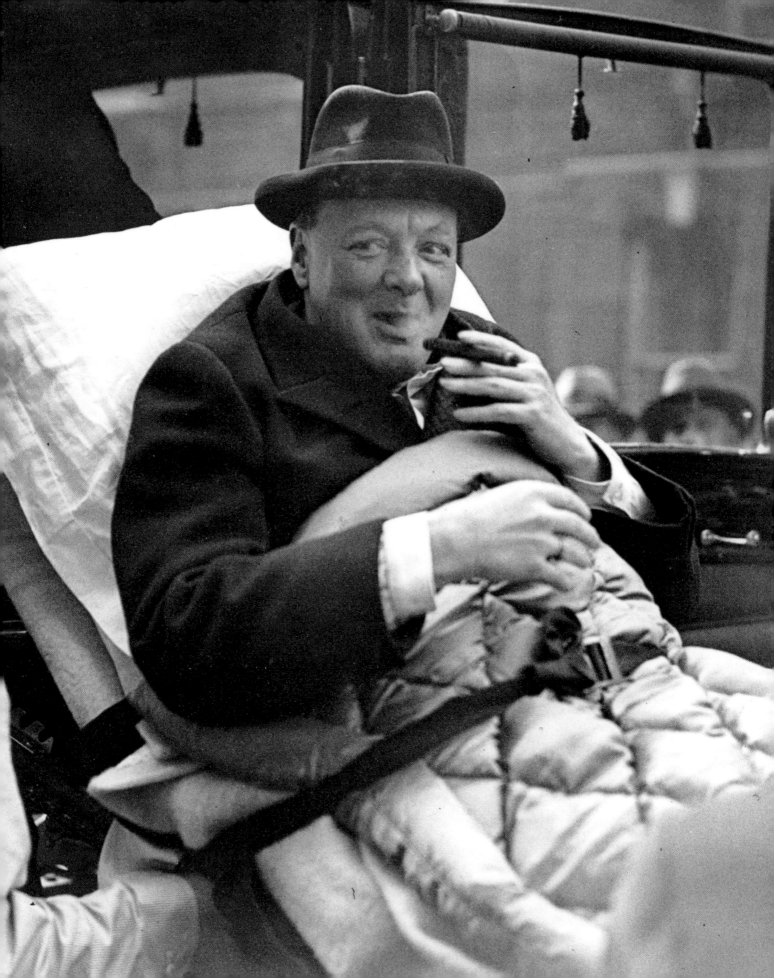

Britain, ill prepared, and Germany, bristling with armaments, were once more at war.

Chamberlain offered Churchill the position he had held from 1911 to 1915, that of First Lord of the Admiralty. A signal was flashed immediately to the Fleet: 'Winston is back'.

As a member of the War Cabinet Churchill immediately pressed for offensive action. He wanted an attack by land and air on the Siegfried Line, the German western defences, in order to relieve German pressure on the

Poles. But no action was taken. He wanted to stop the Swedish iron-ore traffic from the Norwegian port of Narvik and thence through Norwegian territorial waters to Germany, proposing to mine the Norwegian waters in order to force the ships into the open sea where they could be sunk. The Cabinet prevaricated, concerned over infringing Norwegian neutrality.

But if all was quiet on the Western Front, little happening in the air and German ships

With his daughter Diana arriving at St Ethelburga's Church, Bishopsgate, London, for her marriage to Duncan Sandys MP, 16 September 1935.

With Neville Chamberlain, Prime Minister at the outbreak of the Second World War. Chamberlain's policies were blamed for many of the defeats suffered during the first months of conflict. In May 1940 he resigned, leaving Churchill to fulfil his destiny.

safely hugging the Norwegian coast, Churchill ensured that within his own sphere of authority the war was waged with all the intensity possible. Submarines were being sunk. A convoy system was instituted for merchant ships. The German pocket-battleship *Graf Spee* was hunted down in December 1939 by three British cruisers which, though outgunned, forced her to take refuge in Montevideo where she was scuttled.

Determined to deny Germany ready access to Swedish iron ore, Churchill, in mid-September, proposed an expedition to Narvik and an advance into Sweden to occupy the ore fields. He proposed 29 December as the day for action. At the end of the year when no agreement on action had been reached he proposed seizing the ore-carrying ships on 4 January, warning that if there was further delay, 'the Germans might attempt to forestall us'. Still hesitating, the War Cabinet decided in mid-January that for the moment no action would be taken to interrupt the traffic from Narvik.

Full of offensive ideas Churchill suggested dropping mines from aircraft into the Rhine to disrupt a main supply route within Germany. This was vetoed by the Air Ministry who replied that the scheme was 'unprofitable'. Churchill commented in the margin of their letter, 'Don't irritate them dear!' The situation in the War Cabinet was not far removed from that which faced Churchill in 1914: there were

Neville Chamberlain (1869–1940)

Neville Chamberlain became Prime Minister in 1937 and was at the forefront of the movement to appease Hitler in the latter years of the 1930s. A sincere man, on his return from a meeting with Hitler in 1938, he told the crowds in Downing Street, '... peace with honour. I believe it is peace for our time,' but less than a year later he had to announce to the British public that 'this country is at war with Germany'.

Reverses in the first months of the war – notably in Norway – led to widespread criticism of Chamberlain's management. He resigned as Prime Minister in May 1940. His chosen successor was Lord Halifax, but Halifax declined. This left Churchill as the only alternative. Chamberlain, already suffering from ill health, remained leader of the Conservative Party until a month before his death on 9 November 1940.

three separate services with no proper co-ordination and no one with both knowledge and authority to exercise it. Frustrated, Churchill wrote on 15 January to Lord Halifax, the Foreign Secretary, who as Lord Irwin had been Viceroy of India at the time of the India Bill, 'of the awful difficulties which our machinery of war-conduct presents to positive action'.

A few days later he made his fourth broad-cast of the war, his words inspiring millions of people in Britain, France and through clandestine radios in the German occupied countries. 'Let the great cities of Warsaw, of Prague, of Vienna banish despair in the midst of their agony. Their liberation is sure. The day will come when the joybells will ring again throughout Europe'.

In February 1940 Churchill personally wrote the order to board a German merchant ship, which had taken refuge in Norwegian territorial waters, and rescue the 299 British prisoners on board, mostly from ships the *Graf Spee* had sunk. One week later he welcomed home the crews of the cruisers which had forced the *Graf Spee* to scuttle itself. Theirs had been a brilliant action, 'In a dark, cold winter it had warmed the cockles of the British heart'. Already, after only a few months of the war, Churchill was sounding and looking like the only man with the qualities needed to lead the nation. Even Halifax, a long-time critic noted, 'What an extraordinary creature he is. It is the combination of simplicity, energy and intellectual agility that is so entertaining'.

In late March 1940 the War Cabinet agreed Churchill's plan to mine Norwegian waters and occupy Narvik. On 4 April Chamberlain said publicly that Hitler had 'missed the bus' but when the mining of Norwegian waters began on 8 April it became embarrassingly clear that it was Chamberlain who had missed the bus. The Germans were at that moment landing in Norway, occupying Narvik the following day. Ten German destroyers were sunk but, having

air superiority, the Germans could not be dislodged. On 7 May Parliament debated the Norwegian situation. Churchill loyally defended the government's position, his listeners being unaware that, had his advice been taken, the Germans would have been forestalled. Lloyd George pleaded with him 'not to allow himself to become an air-raid shelter to keep the splinters from hitting his colleagues'. The blame was seen to fall squarely on Chamberlain and there were many calls for him to resign. He clung on, but when he sought to preserve national unity by inviting Labour and Liberals into government, their leaders declared that they would serve only under another Prime Minister.

There were two contenders as Chamberlain's successor: Halifax and Churchill. The Conservative party at large preferred Halifax who was also Chamberlain's choice when the three men, together with the government Chief Whip, David Margesson, met in Chamberlain's office on 9 May. Halifax demurred on the grounds that as a peer he would be unable to guide events from the House of Lords. With Churchill as a natural war leader dominating the Commons that would undoubtedly have been true. Chamberlain reluctantly accepted this, as did Churchill with less reluctance. The die seemed cast. The following morning Hitler launched his blitzkrieg into Holland, Belgium and France. For a few hours Chamberlain thought he should remain at the helm while the battle raged in France but opinion from every quarter was against him and he advised the King to send for Churchill.

Churchill's months of frustration were over. At 65 he had become Prime Minister in the most daunting situation imaginable, yet he was 'conscious of a profound sense of relief' as he went to bed at 3am in the early hours of 11 May. 'At last I had authority to give directions over the whole scene. I felt as if I were walking with destiny and all my past life had been but a preparation for this hour and this trial. I could not be reproached either for making the war or with want of preparation for it. I thought I knew a good deal about it, and I was sure I would not fail'.

Door to No. 10 Downing Street. Churchill first walked through this door as Prime Minister in May 1940.

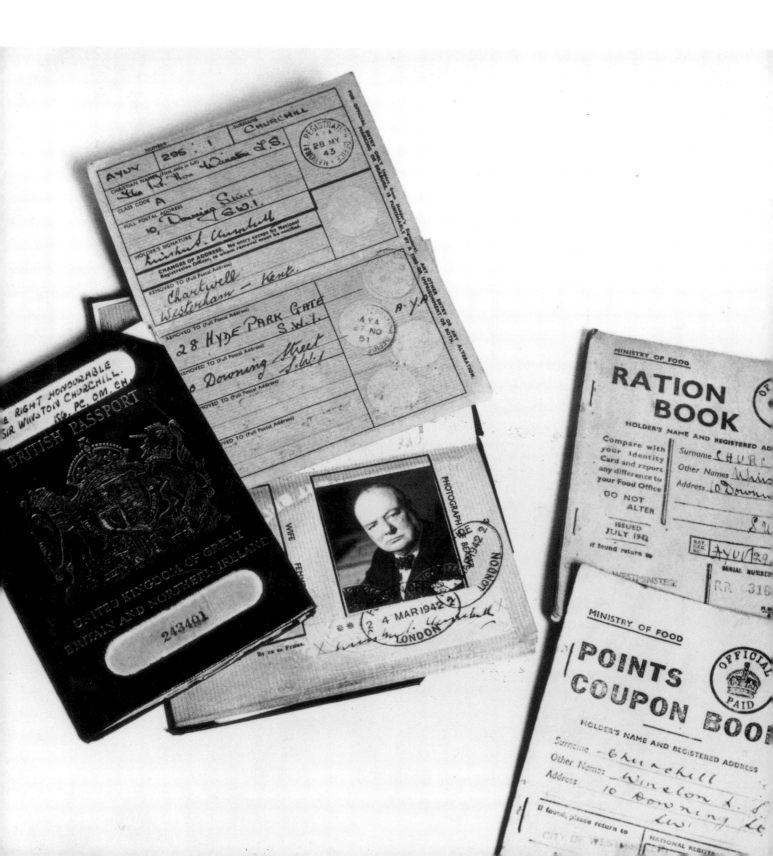

Churchill inspecting bomb damage in Ramsgate, August 1940.

4

WAR LEADER 1940–45

The lessons Churchill had learned from the disastrous Dardanelles campaign a quarter of a century before, and which had been reinforced by the lackadaisical conduct of the war so far, now bore fruit. Upon becoming Prime Minister he immediately appointed himself Minister of Defence, a post which had hitherto not existed (but which has been seen ever since as essential). For the first time in two world wars Britain had at the helm a statesman expert in the art of war. At last all the strings came together in one hand. As a colonel on the staff wrote, 'We were now going to get direction, leadership, action with a snap in it!'

Churchill also chaired the Cabinet and the smaller War Cabinet. Thus, political and military views were co-ordinated at the highest level. Strategy was directly translated into plans that were promptly implemented with the appropriate resources. Industrial needs could be balanced against those of the armed forces. Men could be directed where required. Churchill embraced all aspects of the war. He was still accountable to his Cabinet and to Parliament but he had acquired more power than is usual in the British democracy. He acknowledged this with the explanation, 'This

was really necessary because times were so very bad. It was accepted because everyone knew how near death and ruin we were'.

In creating a national government Churchill brought in the foremost members of all parties. Former opponents became colleagues in arms. Attlee, the leader of the Labour opposition, became Lord Privy Seal and a member of the War Cabinet. (In February 1942 he would become Deputy Prime Minister.) Ernest Bevin – a thorn in Churchill's side during his Russian venture – became Minister of Labour and National Service. Lloyd George was offered the Ministry of Agriculture but declined, no longer confident that Britain would survive. Churchill as Prime Minister would normally have become leader of his party but, conscious that he had not been the first choice of most Conservatives and had some way to go before he would gain their confidence, the ailing Chamberlain was left as leader of the party until he resigned a month before his death on 9 November 1940. For similar reasons Churchill suppressed any doubts about Halifax whom he left as Foreign Secretary.

With the ruffling of some Conservative feathers most of the senior posts in government

Churchill's wartime cabinet, October 1941. From front row, left to right, Sir John Anderson, Churchill, Clement Attlee, Anthony Eden; back row, Arthur Greenwood, Ernest Bevin, Lord Beaverbrook and Sir Kingsley Wood.

Clement Attlee

1st Earl Attlee

Clement Attlee was the first Labour Prime Minister to serve a full term as Prime Minister and, to date, the longest serving leader of the Labour Party.

Born in 1883, Attlee was educated at Haileybury and University College, Oxford. Trained as a lawyer, he joined the Labour Party in 1908. He became a lecturer at the London School of Economics in 1913 but enlisted the following year on the outbreak of the First World War during which he was seriously wounded and reached the rank of major. He became, in 1919, the mayor of the London borough of Stepney and in 1922 entered Parliament. In 1924 he was appointed Parliamentary Private Secretary to Ramsay MacDonald, the first Labour Prime Minister.

Attlee served in the first two Labour governments, as Under-secretary of State for War in 1924, then as Chancellor of the Duchy of Lancaster and later as Postmaster General in the 1929 to 1931 government.

Throughout the 1930s Attlee opposed the policy of appeasement and, having in 1935 been elected leader of the Labour Party, played a significant role in the formation of the coalition government in 1940, where he took on the role of Churchill's deputy in the War Cabinet, the Defence Committee and in Parliament. He was appointed Lord Privy Seal from 1940–42, Deputy Prime Minister 1942–45, Dominions Secretary 1942–43 and Lord President of the Council 1943–45.

Labour was returned to power in a landslide in the General Election which followed victory in Europe in 1945. As Prime Minister, Attlee represented the United Kingdom in the second session of the final Big Three conference at Potsdam in that year. The Labour Government under Attlee began with the clear manifesto of nationalising utilities and the creation of the welfare state. The enactment of all this, which included the establishment of the National Health Service, was substantially achieved. In the international field Attlee's government saw India to inderpendence, the ending of Britain's mandate in Palestine and entry into the Korean War.

When the Conservative Party under Churchill were returned to government in the General Election of 1951, Attlee continued to lead his party in opposition until 1955 when he retired and was elevated to the peerage. He died in 1967.

had been filled by 13 May when Churchill called his ministers together, telling them, 'I have nothing to offer but blood, toil, tears and sweat'. He repeated those words later in the day when, addressing Parliament he declared: 'You ask, what is our policy? I will say it is to wage war, by sea, land and air, with all our might and with all the strength God can give us… You ask, what is our aim? I can answer in one word, victory, victory in spite of all terror, victory, however long and hard the road may be; for without victory there is no survival… But I take up my task with buoyancy and hope. I feel sure that our cause will not be suffered to fail among men. At this time I feel entitled to claim the aid of all, and I say, come then let us go forward together with our united strength.'

Although publicly Churchill exuded confidence, those close to him would later testify to his profound anxiety. General Hastings Ismay, appointed to run his small Defence Office, recalled that, having heard people cheer him in the street, 'He dissolved into tears. "Poor, people," he said, "poor people. They trust me, and I can give them nothing but disaster for quite a long time".'

In France the battle was being lost. On 16 May the Germans broke through the Allied positions at Maastricht, thus outflanking the main French defence, the Maginot Line, constructed over many years. Churchill flew to Paris determined to exert what personal influence he could to stiffen French resolve.

During the next four weeks, as the Germans swept all before them, Churchill would fly to France five times, hazardous journeys which, because of bad weather, were not always escorted by fighters. On one occasion two German fighters flew beneath his small twin-engined aircraft, fortunately without the pilots looking up.

By late May the evacuation of British forces cut off and surrounded at Dunkirk began. Over nine days 186,587 British and 111,000 French troops were rescued from the beaches and brought to Britain by an assembly of every type of craft available, small and large, from open boats to paddle-steamers and naval vessels. Seventy guns were saved but the army had lost a vast amount of war material which would take time to replace. In the air over Dunkirk the Royal Air Force lost only one aircraft for every four German planes shot down but the bigger picture was more sombre. During the previous three weeks the war in France and Flanders had cost the Royal Air Force over 500 aircraft, almost as many as the factories in Britain had turned out in that time, putting back by many months the time when parity in the air would be achieved.

On 4 June 1940, the day the Dunkirk evacuation ended, Churchill told Parliament, 'We shall not flag or fail. We shall go on to the end. We shall fight in France, we shall fight in the seas and oceans, we shall fight with growing confidence and growing strength in the air; we shall defend our Island, whatever the cost may be. We shall fight on the beaches, we shall fight on the landing grounds, we shall fight in the fields and in the streets, we shall fight in the hills; we shall never surrender'. This was the sort of speech which would raise and maintain morale. It was no mere rhetoric. People believed and were inspired, whatever their task, to do their very best. Churchill had no speechwriters; he dictated his own and he meant what he said.

Sir David Low cartoon in the London Evening Standard, *14 May 1940.*

On 31 July 1940 Churchill inspected the coastal fortifications and defence works. He is seen here on a sandbagged gun emplacement with its defenders.

Major General Hastings 'Pug' Ismay
(General The Lord Ismay)

Born in India, Ismay returned there after education in England and served on the North West Frontier before the First World War. He also saw active service in Somaliland before returning to India where he served in a number of important staff appointments.

In 1936 he was made Deputy Secretary to the Committee of Imperial Defence and had become the Secretary by the time Churchill became Prime Minister and Minister of Defence. Ismay's small staff of specially selected officers formed Churchill's Defence Office. As the head of this staff Ismay was in constant intimate communication with Churchill, travelling with him on a number of important occasions including the fateful visit to France before the French capitulation. Churchill wrote of Ismay and his staff, 'My debt to them was immeasurable'.

Ismay rose steadily in rank and in 1946 was appointed Chief of Staff to the Viceroy of India, Lord Mountbatten, in the negotiations which led to independence for India. In 1948 he became Chairman of the Festival of Britain Council and in 1951 joined Churchill's third government as Secretary of State for Commonwealth Relations. In 1952 he became the first Secretary General of NATO, retiring in 1957.

The closeness of the relationship between Ismay and Churchill may be judged from a remark made by the latter's doctor, Lord Moran, when suggestions were made in 1952 that Churchill should go to the House of Lords. Moran doubted if anyone had those powers of persuasion, adding, 'Not even Ismay'.

Before Dunkirk the situation had seemed hopeless. General Ismay had thought that no more than 50,000 British troops would be saved. The French were in retreat and the Belgian King was suing for an armistice. It was not surprising that some of those in the know doubted if Britain would survive. It was in this climate that the question arose of Mussolini, the Italian dictator, brokering a settlement to end the fighting. Still hesitating to throw in his lot with Hitler, he might, as a mediator, pick up some crumbs without risk. In the War Cabinet this became a four-day struggle between Halifax and Churchill. Halifax argued

Officers of the Royal Ulster
Rifles awaiting evacuation
at Bray Dunes – about
five miles from Dunkirk,
May 1940.

logically. He had discussed the matter with the French Premier, Paul Reynaud, and thought that Britain and France together would get better terms than after the French had been defeated and Britain was left alone. Churchill, at this stage of the war had no strategic plan but his grasp of history gave him the gut feeling that the British, with their sheer bloody-mindedness and the English Channel as their moat, would prevail.

In the War Cabinet on 28 May Chamberlain thought that nothing would be lost by considering 'decent terms if such were offered'. Attlee warned that once negotiations began 'it would be impossible to rally the morale of the people'. Churchill, understanding that Hitler would have nothing but contempt for a nation which sued for peace, declared that 'nations which went down fighting rose again, but those which surrendered tamely were finished'.

The War Cabinet adjourned and the room then filled with some 25 other ministers whom Churchill had arranged to address. Having explained the grim situation he went on, 'I have thought carefully in these last days whether it was part of my duty to consider entering into negotiations with That Man'. He continued by saying it was idle to think Britain would get better terms if they sued for peace rather than if they fought on. Britain would become a slave state. He ended 'If this long island story of ours is to end at last, let it end only when each of us lies choking in his own

blood upon the ground'. There was spontaneous approval. As one senior Minister noted, no one left one of Churchill's Cabinet meetings without feeling a braver man. Churchill now had the mandate he needed to tell the War Cabinet that there would be no further thought of negotiations. Britain would fight on. Her theatres of operations were about to increase for on 10 June Mussolini declared war. The Mediterranean was now a hostile sea and the border between Egypt and the Italian colony of Libya a new battlefront.

The French declared Paris an open city, the Government moving into the country as the Germans drove through France. Churchill still hoped that France would continue to resist and even as the evacuation proceeded from Dunkirk plans for reinforcements to cross the Channel further west were being made. On 12 June, having just returned from his fourth visit to France, Churchill took a telephone call from Reynaud who asked for his immediate return. On the following morning, at Hendon aerodrome, Churchill was told the weather was too bad for flying. 'To hell with that', he replied. 'I'm going, whatever happens! This is too serious a situation to bother with the weather!' He sent for his heavy pistol saying, 'If we are attacked on the way I may be able to kill at least one German'.

Accompanied by General Ismay, Beaverbrook, Halifax and others, he landed at an abandoned airfield. There was no one to meet

Churchill raises his hat from his car in Bristol, April 1941.

Inspecting Polish troops.

Brendan Bracken
Viscount Bracken of Christchurch

Born in Kilmanock in Ireland in 1901, Brendan Bracken was educated at a Jesuit college before being sent to work in Australia.

Moving to London he joined the publishing world, becoming a director of Eyre & Spottiswood, an editor of various publications before being promoted to managing director of the *Economist* in 1928. By now he had become a close friend of Churchill whom he helped in his election campaigns during the 1920s before being himself elected to Parliament in 1929.

His contribution to British politics is best summed up in the letter Churchill wrote in 1940 to King George VI's private secretary: 'Mr Bracken is a Member of Parliament of distinguished standing and exceptional ability. He has sometimes been my sole supporter in the years when I have been striving to get this country properly defended, especially from the air. He has suffered as I have done every form of official hostility. Had he joined the ranks of time-servers and careerists who were assuring the public that our Air Force was larger than that of Germany, I have no doubt that he would have long ago attained High Office.'

Bracken was appointed to the Privy Council, was a very successful Minister of Information from 1941 before becoming First Lord of the Admiralty in 1945. Created viscount in 1952, he died of cancer in 1958.

them so he commandeered a car, saying to his companions, 'Well, the journey does not promise well. Do you not think that a good luncheon is in order?' But lunch was not so easy to obtain as Churchill later recalled, 'We found a café, which was closed, but after explanations we obtained a meal'. He was upbeat when the French premier appeared but the French were too deeply demoralised for Churchill's advocacy to prevent their surrender. Reynaud was sure the Germans would invade Britain. 'What will you do when they come?' he asked. 'If they swim we will drown them. If they land we will *frappez* them *sur la tête*,' Churchill replied.

As Churchill and his colleagues flew back he was by no means downcast. In good humour he turned to Ismay and said, 'Do you realise

we probably have a maximum of three months to live?' Then he slept. As he later wrote, 'This was wise for there was a long way to go before bed time'.

On 18 June, the day after France sought an armistice, Churchill spoke in Parliament of the ordeal ahead. He first dismissed any thought of an inquest into past affairs. 'Of this I am quite sure, if we open a quarrel between the past and the present, we shall find we have lost the future.' Then, moving to the immediate future, he expected the Battle for Britain was about to begin. 'Upon this battle depends the survival of Christian civilisation… Hitler knows that he will have to break us in this island or lose the war.' He concluded, in just over half an hour, with the stirring words: 'Let us therefore brace ourselves to our duties and so bear ourselves that, if the British Empire and its Commonwealth last for a thousand years, men will still say, "This was their finest hour".'

Later in the day Churchill was persuaded to broadcast the same speech to millions of listeners. He was always at his best in Parliament, but those who heard both speeches thought he sounded tired in the second. Outwardly he was the epitome of confidence but the huge anxieties he was bearing were taking their toll and just over a week later his wife warned him that he was being unnecessarily brusque with some of his colleagues.

The northern part of France was now occupied by the Germans who left the southern

Top: 'Southern England 1944. Spitfires attacking flying bombs' by Sir Walter Thomas Monnington.

Bottom: On 30 June 1944, as Hitler's 'secret weapon', the V-1 flying bomb, was causing death and destruction in London, Churchill and Clementine visited their daughter Mary's anti-aircraft battery in Kent, to observe the defences.

part under the French government which had concluded the armistice. There was grave concern in Britain over the future of French warships at Oran in French North Africa. If these powerful ships fell into German hands they would significantly affect the balance of power at sea. The French were given the option of siding with the Royal Navy, sailing to the West Indies or scuttling themselves. When none of these solutions were accepted, the Royal Navy opened fire. In a ten-minute action on 3 July some 1,200 unfortunate French sailors perished. It had been a hard decision to fire on men who until a few weeks before had been allies, but Oran was a signal to the world of Britain's ruthless determination. When Churchill spoke in Parliament the following day the whole House rose and cheered. The Conservative Party's reservations over their Prime Minister were fading.

Oran also removed some of the American President's reservations. President Roosevelt began to sense that Britain was worth backing. Churchill, knowing that it would be virtually impossible for Britain to defeat Germany unaided, needed American assistance and to this end had argued that this would also be in America's own interests. However, Roosevelt was wary of becoming involved in Britain's struggle. He was shortly up for re-election and had to take into account that the American opinion was generally isolationist. Moreover, the American ambassador in London, Joseph

*Winston and Clementine on
the Thames, viewing bomb
damage to the docks on 25
September 1940.*

Kennedy, continually advised that Britain was finished.

A fortnight after Oran, America agreed to manufacture 14,000 aircraft for Britain during the coming 21 months. Other agreements covered a mass of additional war material. But Roosevelt would still not release the 50 old American mothballed destroyers which Churchill had previously asked for to boost the war against German submarines which were sinking merchant ships at an alarming rate. The ocean was Britain's lifeline; if the U-boats won the Battle of the Atlantic, Britain would starve. Churchill persisted, and Roosevelt relented in August when he offered the use of British bases in Newfoundland, Bermuda, the Bahamas and West Indies in return.

Churchill continued to nurture his close relationship with Roosevelt. He made it plain that Britain could not afford to pay for all that was needed in fighting for what was a common cause. From his speech intended for American listeners came the famous phrase, 'Give us the tools and we will finish the job'. The end result was Lend-Lease under which, from March 1941, America produced armaments for British use.

The Battle of France being over, the Battle of Britain began. Hitler knew he had to defeat the Royal Air Force in order to gain mastery of the skies over the Channel and Southern England before he could launch an invasion of Britain. From mid-August to mid-September German

Churchill is credited with the invention of this label. Documents were graded and labelled according to their urgency. Memoranda issued by Churchill were known as 'prayers'.

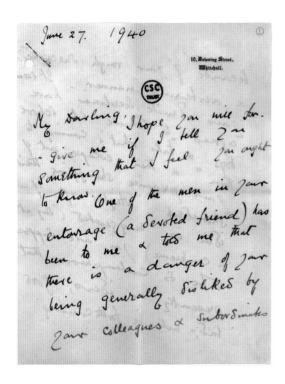

June 27, 1940   **10 Downing Street, Whitehall**

My Darling,

I hope you will forgive me if I tell you something that I feel you ought to know.

One of the men in your entourage (a devoted friend) has been to me & told me that there is a danger of your being generally disliked by your colleagues & subordinates because of your rough sarcastic & overbearing manner. It seems your Private Secretaries have agreed to behave like school boys & 'take what's coming to them' then escape out of your presence shrugging their shoulders – Higher up, if an idea is suggested (say at a conference) you are supposed to be so contemptuous that presently no ideas, good & bad, will be forthcoming. I was astonished & upset because in all these years I have been accustomed to all those who have worked with & under you – I said this & and I was told 'No doubt it's the strain'.

My darling Winston, I must confess that I have noticed a deterioration in your manner; & you are not so kind as you need to be.

It is for you to give the orders & if they are bungled – except for the King, the Archbishop of Canterbury & the Speaker – you can sack anyone & everyone. Therefore with this terrific power you must combine urbanity, kindness & if possible Olympic calm. You used to quote: '*On ne règne sur les âmes que par le calme*' [one reigns over souls only through calm] – I cannot bear that those who serve the country & yourself should not love you as well as admire and respect you.

Besides you won't get the best results by irascibility & rudeness. They will breed either dislike or a slave mentality (Rebellion in war ... being out of the question!).

Please forgive your loving devoted & watchful Clemmie
I wrote this at Chequers last Sunday, tore it up, but here it is now.

Above: A letter from Clementine to Churchill warning him about the 'deterioration' in his manner towards his colleagues.

bombers struck dockyards, factories and air-fields, while German and British fighters filled the skies above Sussex and Kent, their patterns of white condensation trails in the blue summer sky mapping the course of deadly combat.

The Royal Air Force remained in command of the skies and the German invasion was off. On 20 August, at the height of the battle, Churchill paid a tribute to the fighter pilots with the immortal words, 'Never in the field of human conflict has so much been owed by so many to so few'. The words had first been

Elizabeth Nel
(one of Churchill's secretaries during the war)

When he was preparing the production speech, which I think was the longest he ever made in the House of Commons, he instructed me to go outside – we were at Chequers – to get some fresh air into my lungs, because we were going to work late that night. So I did and then he said to me, 'Shorthand', so I sat down and waited. For a little while he walked around, puffing at his cigar and taking it out and putting it in again, and once he threw himself into an armchair and sat there a little while thinking. Then he got up and started dictating, and I wrote and wrote and wrote.

He went on and on, walking round and round the table. Sometimes there would be an emotional note in his voice, especially when speaking about the Royal Navy. And sometimes his voice would drop half an octave and there would be a harsh note, 'That bad man,' he would say, speaking of Hitler. And sometimes, as the force of what he wanted to put across took over, his hands would start gesturing in that way that one got to know so well whenever he was dictating. Sometimes he'd put his thumbs into his waistcoat, sometimes he would lift his finger up and his voice would rise and fall according to what he was saying and it was all very inspiring.

We went on and on and after a bit he swung round on me and said, 'Are you tired?' I said, 'No, no, I'm not tired because I was getting steamed up too, 'We must go on, like the gun horses, until we drop'.

Time went on and I heard a sleepy note coming into his voice and then all of a sudden he dropped the histrionics. He sounded dead level again and he said, ' That's enough for tonight. You can go to bed'. It was half-past four.

Portrait of Churchill by
Frank Salisbury.

Churchill began wearing
these zip-up one-piece
suits, which his family
christened 'rompers',
during the 1930s. He had
them made in a variety of
colours and materials.
In Britain, people began
to copy this Churchillian
fashion.

He did everything... Churchill at the controls of the Boeing Clipper flying boat during his return from America, January 1942.

General Sir Alan Brooke

(Field Marshal the Viscount Alanbrooke of Brookeborough)

Born in 1883 and brought up in France, Alan Brooke completed his education at the Royal Military Academy and was commissioned into the Royal Artillery. By the end of the First World War he was a lieutenant colonel with a Distinguished Service Order and Bar, a Croix de Guerre and six mentions in despatches. Marked for high command he progressed through a succession of appointments from which he emerged with a diversity of experience unrivalled in the British Army.

His consummate performance during the retreat to Dunkirk in 1940 resulted in him being sent back to France within 48 hours to command the 150,000 troops still remaining there. Refusing to sacrifice military principles to political considerations he extricated this force and brought it back to England; in the words of Churchill, 'with singular firmness and dexterity, in circumstances of unimaginable difficulty and confusion'.

In 1941 he was appointed Chief of the Imperial General Staff and Chairman of the Chiefs of Staff Committee which advised Churchill, who was both Prime Minister and Minister of Defence, on issues of strategy and policy. Under the direction of General Sir Alan Brooke, as he then was, this committee became an instrument for directing a vast and complex war machine.

General Brooke was in daily consultation with Churchill, accompanied him to his conferences with Roosevelt and Stalin, and played a leading part in persuading the American Chiefs of Staff to accept the strategy which, in succession, secured the Mediterranean and led to the invasion of France in 1944.

In the face of Churchill's courage, vision and plethora of ideas, Brooke brought a steadying influence. He ensured that military decisions were taken only by those responsible for their implementation. Largely unknown to the public, General Alan Brooke's role in turning the tide when Britain stood alone and later in the final victory was second only to that of Winston Churchill.

heard by General Ismay when Churchill, deeply moved, left Fighter Command's operations room four days before.

Having lost the Battle of Britain, the German Air Force now turned its fury upon London. Throughout September some 200 bombers attacked London each night. Other towns and cities were also hit. People spent nights in the tube stations, street shelters or corrugated steel Anderson shelters which they had dug into their back gardens. The Blitz continued unabated through the winter of 1940–41 but civilian morale held up even though large areas were devastated with 42,000 civilians having been killed or wounded in the nine months of the Blitz. Churchill regularly visited the devastated areas. Seeing him in tears one woman called out, 'See he really cares'. He

was cheered even by those who had been bombed out. 'Give it 'em back!' was the popular cry. The Royal Air Force was returning the punishment but it would be some time before Bomber Command had the resources to mount heavy and effective raids.

On 19 March there was a particularly heavy raid on London while Churchill was giving dinner for the emissaries Roosevelt had sent across. He took them up to the roof where, as they watched the fireworks, he recited poetry:

Hear the heavens filled with shouting,
and there rain'd a ghastly dew
From the nation's airy navies
grappling in the central dew.

Churchill often donned his tin hat and watched the air raids from the roof. On one occasion someone came up and asked him if he would mind moving. When Churchill asked why, he was told, 'Because you are sitting on the chimney and smoking out the people below'.

Much has been written about Churchill's method of work, often critical. It was certainly unusual. It enabled him to cover an immense field and without doubt no other leader matched his performance. He was able to comprehend the large picture while at the same time being fully aware of the smallest details. He demanded details not to interfere but to warn him when he needed to interfere. If he persisted in argument it was to get to the truth. He generated ideas by the score, often absorbing time in discussion which others could barely afford. Ismay said five out of twenty were good, but some of those became war-winners. Nothing escaped his notice and many of the technical and scientific break-throughs were due to his interest and drive.

His instructions were always in the form of memoranda, letters or telegrams with an 'Action this Day' red tab on those of immediate priority. He expected his immediate staff to be instantly available at all hours and if he was sometimes gruff in manner he always expressed appreciation afterwards.

His previous wide experience of war at various levels was both a blessing and a bane to the Chiefs of Staff. No other political leader could meet his military advisers on virtually equal terms. It is interesting that in 1941 Churchill wrote; 'Renown awaits the commander who restores artillery to its prime importance on the battlefield'. (This was 18 months before General Montgomery's massed artillery paved the way for success at Alamein.) The Chiefs of Staff came around to his point of view or he to theirs often only after a good deal of argument, not always in the best of humour, but he never overruled them.

General Sir Alan Brooke, the Chairman of the Chiefs of Staff who bore the brunt of the wearying arguments, made scathing entries in his late night diaries which were published after his death, but acknowledged that Churchill was indispensable, his leadership far

Bletchley Park

Bletchley Park, located in Buckinghamshire was the wartime home of British code-breaking. Employing over 1,000 men and women, its mission was to crack the German codes used to transmit orders and intelligence, notably to read the messages enciphered by the apparently impenetrable electro-mechanical Enigma machine. The capture of an Enigma machine from a sinking U-boat, information supplied to the British by Poland, and the repetitive nature of much traffic, enabled a breakthrough. From July 1940, such vital information as advanced warning of Luftwaffe raids, details of the whereabouts of U-boats in the Atlantic and German troop movements on various fronts became available. The cracking of the Enigma cipher can truly be described as one of the turning points in the war.

A selection of Enigma messages went frequently to Churchill in a buff-coloured box of which he alone in Downing Street had the key. The 'geese who laid the golden eggs and never cackled' was his description of deciphering staff.

The Family at War

Early in 1941 Clementine became President of the Young Women's Christian Association (YWCA) Wartime Fund and later in that year took on the Chairmanship of the Red Cross Aid to Russia Fund. In 1946 she was awarded the Grand Cross of the Order of the British Empire.

All four of Churchill's surviving children served in the armed forces during the Second World War. Diana initially served in the Women's Royal Naval Service (The Wrens) but with three small children and her husband, Duncan Sandys, invalided out of the army she completed the war in the St John's Ambulance Service. Randolph was commissioned into his father's old regiment, the 4th Hussars, served with the commandos in North Africa and parachuted into Yugoslavia as a member of the British Military Mission. Sarah joined the Women's Auxiliary Air Force (WAAF) and Mary served with the Women's Auxiliary Territorial Service (ATS). Both Sarah and Mary accompanied their father on his wartime journeys.

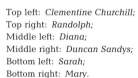

Top left: *Clementine Churchill;*
Top right: *Randolph;*
Middle left: *Diana;*
Middle right: *Duncan Sandys;*
Bottom left: *Sarah;*
Bottom right: *Mary.*

outweighing his faults. Brooke, in a foreword to Arthur Bryant's *Turn of the Tide* writes, 'He is quite the most wonderful man I have ever met'. Part of Brooke's burden was Churchill's inordinately long working day. It began with breakfast in bed where, attended by staff and secretaries, he stayed working on papers, dictating correspondence until it was time to bath and get up for lunch, or earlier if there was a War Cabinet or other appointment. Late afternoon or early evening he would sleep for an hour before a second bath and a big dinner with champagne, visitors and talk of war. After dinner there was sometimes a film but it was always down to work again, perhaps a late-night discussion and invariably further dictation to the relays of secretaries always on hand with their typewriters which had been silenced in order not to interrupt his train of thought. Bed would come some time in the early hours.

It was the short afternoon rest which, recharging his batteries, enabled him to cram so much into one day. Consistent with his philosophy that man needs a change rather than a rest, Churchill and his whole entourage moved to Chequers, the Prime Minister's official country house, at the weekends. Here work continued, leavened with visitors of all sorts.

The Battle of the Atlantic was Churchill's longest and biggest worry. In early 1941 half a million tons of shipping were sunk in a three

month period. He later wrote, 'This mortal danger to our lifeline gnawed my bowels'. British code-breakers working on German naval signals played a vital part in the battle; Churchill called them 'the geese who laid my golden eggs'. It would not be until mid-1943 that the battle was won and even then the dangers lurked sporadically beneath the waves, requiring constant vigilance.

Churchill with his daughter Mary.

Franklin Delano Roosevelt
(1882–1945)

First elected president in 1933,
Roosevelt remains the only man in
US history to be re-elected four
times. Although at the start of the
war public opinion in America was
for strict neutrality, Roosevelt did
what he could to help Britain,
notably with the Lend-Lease
arrangement which provided
armaments which Britain could
neither produce herself in sufficient
quantity nor afford to purchase from
America.

From a meeting between Roosevelt
and Churchill in 1941 came the
'Atlantic Charter' which linked the
two nations. The Japanese attack on
Pearl Harbor and Hitler's declaration
of war brought America into the war.
From then on Roosevelt, Churchill
and Stalin formed the 'Big Three' to
debate war strategy.

For the last 24 years of his life
Roosevelt suffered from polio.
He died in April 1945, three weeks
before the German surrender.
Churchill and Roosevelt laid the
foundations of the Special
Relationship between Britain and
the US which continues to this day.

One bright episode during these dark days
was the success of British and Commonwealth
forces in the Middle East where the Italians
had been driven from Eritrea and the Libyan
province of Cyrenaica. But it was short lived as
the Germans reinforced the Axis forces in
Libya and by May 1941, under General Erwin
Rommel, they were again in Egypt.

There was worse news from Greece. In
March the War Cabinet had taken the very
difficult decision to send forces which could be
ill spared from Egypt to face the growing
German threat to Greece. There was no great
hope of saving Greece but to let it fall without a
fight would have adverse repercussions else-
where in the Balkans, particularly Yugoslavia.
When battle was joined the Germans in overwhelming strength rapidly drove south and the
Commonwealth forces, predominantly
Australian and New Zealand, faced a week-
long gruelling evacuation from the shores and
coves of Greece. Under constant dive-bomber
attack, 26 ships, including five hospital ships,
were sunk. Although 50,000 men got away
11,000 were taken prisoner.

With hindsight we can see that the effort had
not been entirely futile, quite apart from the
positive message it sent to the partisans in
Yugoslavia. The Germans had been made to
fight for Greece. Had they been allowed a
walk-over they would have had more forces
available for their coming invasion of Russia
and might not then have been halted short of

Moscow in the winter campaign ahead, but
that is only conjecture. What is certain is that
when the Germans broke their non-aggression
treaty and invaded Russia on 22 June 1941,
Britain was no longer alone.

Within 24 hours of the invasion of Russia,
Churchill broadcast to the nation. 'No one
has been a more consistent opponent of
Communism,' he said. 'I will unsay no word I
have spoken about it. But all this fades away
before the spectacle now unfolding… Any man
or state who fights on against Nazism will have
our aid. We shall give whatever help we can to
Russia.'

For the present there was little military
action that Churchill could order to take the
pressure off Russia other than to have the
Royal Air Force intensify its raids on the
German forces in northern France. But the fact
that Britain herself was still short of aircraft
and armaments did not prevent the early
dispatch of military aid to Russia. The inclusion

of 200 fighter aircraft, 60 of which were from American manufacture, was an indication of Churchill's resolve to help. An additional benefit was the passing of intelligence which resulted from British code breakers decrypting German signal traffic on the Russian Front. Its source could not be disclosed and Stalin gave little credit to it.

He would remain a difficult ally, partly through a lack of understanding but also because he cared only for the Russian cause. He pressed for a Second Front to be opened in northern France without showing any understanding that the resources required would take two years to assemble. On other aspects it seemed he simply ignored the facts and there were few, if any, thanks. One convoy to Russia in 1942 lost 23 of its 34 merchant ships and two thirds of its valuable cargo in the Arctic waters, but the Russian leader only complained when

From the deck of HMS Prince of Wales, Churchill watches the destroyer USS McDougal departing with the President on board after the Placentia conference.

Churchill gives the Victory sign in reply to good wishes from sailors and airmen as he disembarks the SS Queen Mary *on arrival in the USA, 1943.*

as a result convoy arrangements came under review. Throughout the war Churchill did all he could to maintain good relations with Stalin but never lost sight of the Russian leader's long-term policy of ending the war in a dominant position.

With Russia involved the war had taken a fresh turn and Churchill decided on a face-to-face meeting with Roosevelt. In August 1941 he sailed in the battleship *Prince of Wales* for a meeting in Newfoundland. From this came great improvements in the arrangements for American aid, including help to Russia, and the Atlantic Charter under which both Britain and the United States pledged themselves

to 'respect the rights of all peoples to choose the form of government under which they will live.'

It was a disappointment to Churchill that the President had told the American people that they were no nearer to war and had shied away from sending a warning to an increasingly hostile Japan. Although it was now unlikely that the war would be lost, winning it was an entirely different matter. Without the United States taking an active part it might drag on 'for another five years and civilisation and culture would be wiped out'. Churchill wondered if Roosevelt understood the risk of remaining out of the war.

The decision was abruptly taken out of American hands on 7 December 1941. In a ferocious attack on Pearl Harbor in Hawaii, Japanese aircraft destroyed three American battleships at their moorings and left 2,400 Americans dead. With this single stroke Japan had achieved naval supremacy in the Far East. Simultaneously Japanese forces were invading Malaya and Hong Kong.

Churchill made immediate plans to leave for another meeting with Roosevelt but before he sailed on 12 December he learned that the British battlecruiser *Repulse* and battleship *Prince of Wales* had been sunk by an air attack off the coast of Malaya. Apart from this disastrous news, he was personally touched by the loss of many of the ship's crew with whom he had sailed four months before. Roosevelt,

7 December 1941: the Japanese bombing of Pearl Harbor in Hawaii brings the United States into the war.

Patrick Kinna
(one of Churchill's private secretaries during the war)

One morning when I had accompanied Churchill on a visit to the White House, the valet, Mr Sawyers, came along to my room to say, 'The Prime Minister wants to dictate. He's in the bathroom – will you go along'. So I went along, completely dressed of course, and there he was like a big porpoise, in the bath going up and down in the water, and he started dictating in between splashes. Then he got out of the bath and wouldn't give the valet much opportunity to dry him, he wanted to get back to his bedroom. He couldn't put a dressing gown on because he was too wet, so he just had a bath towel wrapped around him. I was behind him and he was continuing to dictate as he walked to his bedroom. Then he was walking up and down, just with the bath towel on, and in no time that had come off. I didn't think anything about it really, until there was a rat-a-tat-tat on the door and he said, 'Come in'. He hated being interrupted, so he didn't say it in a very polite way, but in sailed President Roosevelt. And there was Winston completely nude and he said to the President, 'You see, Mr President, I have nothing to hide from you'.

occupied with the situation in the Pacific, had no plans to declare war on Germany but, on 11 December, he was dragged into the European war when both Germany and Italy declared war on the United States. As the battleship *Duke of York*, with Churchill and the Chiefs of Staff on board, ploughed through heavy seas towards America, news arrived that the Japanese had attacked Hong Kong.

This American visit brought important strategic decisions. The defeat of Germany would take precedence over the defeat of Japan. A joint Anglo-American landing would be made in French North Africa. American bombers would operate from Britain and other military deployments were agreed. Churchill addressed Congress and, in spite of suffering a mild heart attack, travelled to Canada, where in Ottawa he addressed the Canadian Parliament.

The conference ended on 12 January when Churchill returned to Britain by flying boat. By the end of the 18-hour flight the aircraft was somewhat off course and narrowly missed being fired on by the German anti-aircraft batteries at Brest. Having corrected course the flying boat approached Britain from the direction of France and, when it was detected by radar and thought to be hostile, fighters were sent up to intercept it. The error was discovered in time and Churchill landed safely.

In the course of the next three-and-a-half years Churchill undertook many hazardous journeys to confer with Roosevelt and Stalin, and to visit the war fronts. He made four more return journeys by sea or air across the Atlantic. He flew twice to Moscow and once to Teheran. There were a number of visits to Cairo and to various places along the North African coast and to Morocco. He crossed to Normandy soon after D-Day and later went on into Germany. Italy, Gibraltar, Malta, Greece and Turkey all merited visits.

Churchill's wartime travels fulfilled a number of needs. They were mostly prompted in the first instance by the requirement, as he saw it, to personally influence people and make things happen. These were the logical reasons which would have prompted any ordinary political leader to quit his desk occasionally. But, as we know, Churchill was no ordinary leader. He had reasons of his own. 'A man who has to play an effective part in taking grave and terrible decisions of war may need the refreshment of adventure. He may also need the comfort that when sending so many others to their death he may share in a small way their risks. His fields of personal interest, and consequently his forces of action, are stimulated by direct contact with the event.'

These were days when flying itself could be a risky business, quite apart from the threat of enemy action. Aircraft were less reliable than now, particularly in poor weather. Flying in an unpressurised aircraft, sometimes a draughty converted bomber, also had its medical hazards for Churchill as he was prone to pneumonia.

There were sometimes hostile aircraft about. Twice, once over the Bay of Biscay and once over the Western Desert, aircraft taking the same route as the Prime Minister were shot down with the loss of all aboard.

It took an American legend, General Douglas MacArthur, to put these epic journeys into context, 'If disposal of all the Allied decorations were today placed by Providence in my hands, my first act would be to award the Victoria Cross to Winston Churchill. Not one of those who wear it deserves it more than he. A flight of 10,000 miles through hostile and foreign skies may be the duty of young pilots, but for a Statesman burdened with the world's

cares it is an act of inspiring gallantry and valour'.

In January 1942, with the war going badly, Churchill demanded a vote of confidence to which Parliament responded in his favour by 464 to one. The first half of 1942 brought unremitting disaster. In the Far East, Burma, Malaya, Singapore, the East Indies, the Philippines and many smaller islands fell to the Japanese. In the Western Desert the Axis forces captured Tobruk and drove to within 200 miles of Cairo, taking over 30,000 prisoners. As Churchill boarded his flying boat on 25 June to return from yet another American visit he learned that there was to be a vote of censure

Immediately after the Japanese attack on Pearl Harbor, Churchill travelled to Washington to confer with President Roosevelt. He addressed the US Congress on 26 December 1941, warning them that the Axis powers would 'stop at nothing'.

George Elsey

(Head of Roosevelt's Map Room in the White House, on the occasion of Churchill's visit to Washington in 1943)

I think Churchill very much enjoyed the occasion (of the summit conference with Roosevelt and Stalin, 1943) with his sense of history, thinking of Versailles, the Congress of Vienna and so on – they were the great leaders of the world, meeting together to combat a mortal enemy to free the democratic world – two mortal enemies, of course, Germany and Japan, as they were at that time. Churchill was clearly in his element and you could see and hear this in his rhetoric – I think he loved every moment of it.

Churchill had had laryngitis and lost his voice at the start of the Teheran Conference (in November 1943), but his health seemed to improve as the conference progressed. At the plenary session they were going hammer and tongs at each other and he seemed to be all right.

Of course we only discovered later, in fact after the war, that he had had pneumonia in February of the same year as the Teheran Conference. He got pneumonia again I think a couple of weeks after the conference, so this sore throat or whatever it was must have been leading up to it. Then later on he had a heart attack, so it was prodigious, really, the way he kept his energies, but he did. He must have had the strength of an ox.

Occasionally you felt, when you saw him sitting there – very sturdy, a real bulldog figure – and this was not just at Teheran, this was all the way through – that there was a rather olde worlde courtesy, a magnanimity towards the other two with whom he'd been arguing and towards other people in general. Although he was very business like and could be demanding – well, he was demanding, on everyone who worked for him – he was generous at the same time.

against him in Parliament brought by his critics. It was defeated by 475 votes to 25. In spite of all the setbacks he still had the massive support of the House of Commons.

Concerned that fresh commanders were needed for the battle in the Western Desert, Churchill decided to assess the situation personally and make the necessary changes on the spot. He would fly to Cairo and then go on to Moscow to meet Stalin. Anxious over the Russian leader's reaction when he learned that the Second Front could not be launched before 1943, Churchill felt he must break the news himself. 'It would be,' he said, 'like carrying a lump of ice to the North Pole'. The only doubts about the Prime Minister's immediate travel plans came from the War Cabinet who feared for his health. These he ignored and it became a typical Churchillian journey.

After 21 hours in the air and having stopped to refuel in Gibraltar and Malta, Churchill's party, flying in two converted Liberator bombers, arrived in Cairo in time for breakfast on 3 August. General Sir Alan Brooke, in his diary, noted that Churchill 'turned up delighted with his trip and looking remarkably fresh. He has got his doctor with him who tells me he was a little worried about his pulse'. The same diary entry recorded an event nineteen hours later, 'PM again called me in and kept me up until 1.30am'.

No doubt Churchill had managed his routine siesta, but, even so, he was setting a fast pace

Josef Stalin (1878–1953)

Stalin – meaning 'man of steel' – was a leading Bolshevik and General Secretary of the Communist Party Central Committee. After Lenin's death in 1924 he controlled Russia and ruthlessly disposed of opponents both great and small: from peasants to political enemies who were imprisoned, exiled or shot.

In 1939 Stalin signed a non-aggression pact with Germany, but Hitler invaded Russia in 1941. From that point on Stalin, with Churchill and Roosevelt, was one of the 'Big Three', although by the time of the Tehran Conference in 1943 it was becoming apparent that Russian post-war policy would be at odds with Anglo-American intentions.

The extent of his purges became clear only after his death in 1953, and he was denounced for 'crimes against the party' in 1956.

making far-reaching changes in the high command. Brooke's diary the following day indicated some irritation after a discussion with the Prime Minster at 1.00am followed by a take-off for 8th Army Headquarters in the desert at 4.45am. Churchill, in a humorous observation on the unsuccessful precautions to keep the swarms of flies at bay, remarked that breakfast at the headquarters was taken in 'a wire netted cube full of flies and important military personages'.

Flying on to Moscow Churchill arrived at the Kremlin within two hours of landing. General Brooke's diary records the tense atmosphere in which the talks began. Stung by Stalin's abusive questions and a taunt, 'When are you going to start fighting?' Churchill 'crashed his fist on the table and began one of his wonderful spontaneous orations... and then went on to tell Stalin exactly what his feelings were about fighting'. Without waiting for a translation Stalin replied, 'I do not understand what you are saying but, by God, I like your sentiment'. The three days of talks were often tense but ended with a six-hour banquet so that it was 3.15am by the time Churchill got back to his villa. Two hours later he was airborne.

From Moscow Churchill returned to the Western Desert where General Bernard Montgomery had been appointed to take command. General Brooke's diary for 20 August records a day which had been 'a wonderful example of Winston's vitality...

Called at 6.00am... a bathe in the sea... a very strenuous day touring the front... clouds of sand... long walks between troops... another bathe, contrary to his doctor's orders... rolled over by the wave and did a V-sign with his legs... a drive to the aerodrome and as soon as we emplaned he went to sleep and never woke up until we bumped down the Cairo runway... then followed a conference, dinner... he kept me up until 2.00am... at 7.30am I woke with my bed shaking'. It was the Prime Minister inviting him for breakfast.

One thing which had impressed Stalin was the increasing intensity with which the Royal Air Force was striking Germany. On 30 May the first '1,000 bomber' raid had struck Cologne. The minutes of Churchill's meeting with Stalin recorded the Prime Minister saying that, 'If need be we hoped to shatter almost every dwelling in every German city'. No doubt his actual words were meant to assure Stalin that Britain meant business at a time when bombing was its only means of attacking its principal enemy, but they reflected what had become bombing policy.

The Royal Air Force had earlier attempted to strike precisely at military and industrial targets but the means of delivery were soon seen to be insufficiently accurate for this to be effective. Small specific targets were not profitable, except for certain cases where the additional effort made them worthwhile. To destroy anything it was necessary to saturate the whole

Churchill in a pith helmet viewing the Alamein position, 7 August 1942.

area. Whole cities and towns which supported industry became targets. In the three years that followed the first '1,000 bomber' raid, whole cities were devastated. In the two most severe raids, on Hamburg and Dresden, it is claimed well over 100,000 people were killed. (Hamburg was a port, with shipyards and industry. Dresden, of no industrial significance, had important railway marshalling yards and

the bombing had been requested by the Russians in order to impede German reinforcements moving east). In fulfilling this policy the casualties in Bomber Command were high, some 55,500 aircrew killed and 10,300 aircraft lost. The death rate was proportionally higher even than among the infantry in the First World War.

In the half century since, the policy of area

bombing has evoked much discussion. But without it German war production would have continued unhindered. Even as late as 1943 it required Germany only to resort to 24 hour working to offset the effects of bombing. Area bombing was part of total war; survivors from the bombed parts of London had called out to the Prime Minister, 'Give it 'em back' and people expected Britain to retaliate.

Although approving the policy, Churchill was horrified by the photographs of destruction, 'Are we taking this too far?' he asked in 1943. Perhaps he answered his own question when he said, admittedly in a different context, 'Never maltreat the enemy by halves'. However, by near the end of the war Churchill asked for the policy to be reviewed, writing, 'The destruction of Dresden remains a serious query against the conduct of Allied Bombing'.

On 23 October 1942 came a victory at last. At El Alamein in the Western Desert, General Montgomery's 8th Army inflicted a severe defeat on Rommel's German and Italian forces. On 8 November Anglo-American forces landed in French North Africa. Churchill ordered the church bells to be rung for the first time since the start of the war; hitherto they had been reserved as an invasion warning. 'Now this is not the end,' he warned his listeners at the Lord Mayor's luncheon. 'It is not even the beginning of the end. But it is, perhaps, the end of the beginning.' Meanwhile the Russian army had besieged the Germans in Stalingrad,

With the victorious 8th Army in North Africa.

May 31st, 1944   **Buckingham Palace**

My dear Winston,

I have been thinking a great deal of our conversation yesterday & I have come to the conclusion that it would not be right for either you or I to be where we planned to be on D-Day. I don't think I need emphasize what it would mean to me personally, & to the whole Allied cause, if at this juncture a chance bomb, torpedo or even a mine should remove you from the scene; equally a change of Sovereign at this moment would be a serious matter for the country & Empire. We should both I know love to be there, but in all seriousness I would ask you to reconsider your plan.

Our presence I feel would be an embarrassment to those responsible for fighting the ship or ships in which we were, despite anything we might say to them.

So as I said, I have reluctantly come to the conclusion that the right thing to do is what normally falls to those at the top on such occasions, namely to remain at home & wait. I hope very much that you will see it in this light too. The anxiety of these coming days would be very greatly increased for me if I thought that, in addition to everything else, there was a risk, however remote of my losing your help & guidance.

Believe me
Yours very sincerely
George R.I.

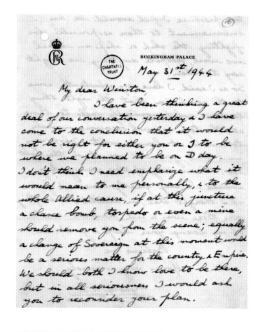

Letter from King George VI pleading with Churchill not to be present at the D-Day landings, June 1944. Churchill agreed, very reluctantly.

which they would regain in February 1943 with the capture of 91,000 prisoners.

During 1943 the tide of war in Europe turned decisively in favour of the Allies. The Russians were on the offensive. The Germans were evicted from North Africa which, said Churchill, was 'To be a springboard and not a sofa,' persuading Roosevelt when they met at Casablanca to support his Mediterranean strategy. This entailed the invasion of Sicily in July and in September, the invasion of Italy. The Italian government had sought an armistice with the Allies after the invasion of Sicily but the stout defence of Italy by the occupying Germans was not affected by the defection of their Italian allies.

Tensions now grew between Churchill and Roosevelt over the effect the Mediterranean strategy was having on the planning and preparations for the cross-channel invasion of France, codenamed 'Overlord', scheduled for 1944. Overlord required the withdrawal of troops and landing craft from the Mediterranean with a consequent slowing down of the advance through Italy.

Roosevelt saw Italy as a sideshow. The European war would be won only through 'Overlord' and the subsequent advance into the heart of Germany. Churchill understood that too but he also divined Stalin's vision of a post-

D-Day, 6 June 1944: the Allied invasion of Normandy was, in Churchill's words at the time, 'undoubtedly the most complicated and difficult operation that has ever taken place'.

Captain Shaw   **A Wartime Visit to France**

(Navigator of the destroyer *Kelvin* during the D-Day landings)

About midnight on 11 June we were called back urgently to Portsmouth. We did not know what was amiss, and it was quite a surprise when we got alongside about 7.30 in the morning and a series of cars came by and out popped Winston Churchill, accompanied by five other very top brass.

As soon as they were on board we set off and proceeded at maximum speed, which was probably about 30 knots, away down the Channel. We had a flag to hoist arranged which told people that Churchill was on board and very stirringly people waved and tooted at us and all the rest of it.

We got across the Channel safely and stopped about half a mile from shore. A picket boat came out and embarked all the top brass, who went ashore. They met Montgomery on the beach. I suppose Churchill was away for two or three hours and when he came back to the ship someone suggested that he might like to have a bash at the enemy. Churchill was delighted and we had to make our way slowly through the water, because we had mines which blew up if we went too near them. We fired on the enemy, so called. I don't know what we were doing or what we were aiming at, but Churchill was very excited indeed. Then happily we came back to the UK safely.

They'd obviously made tremendous news of this as we reached England, because it was all over the national press. It was treated as an adventure trip by Churchill, which was an enormous boost to the national morale.

war Europe with the Balkans firmly in the Russian camp. When hostilities ended he wanted to meet the Russians as far east as possible and a successful Italian campaign with commando assistance to the partisans in the Balkans would be a precursor of that. Roosevelt was barely interested in the shape of post-war Europe; he wanted Germany defeated as soon as possible in order that America could devote its entire effort to finishing the war in the Pacific.

At Casablanca in January, Churchill had got his way but it would be the last time. He travelled to America twice during 1943 and also to the Mediterranean to ensure his strategy was surviving but Roosevelt was now the dominant partner by virtue of the preponderance of American resources. To Roosevelt's voice was added that of Stalin when the 'Big Three' met at Teheran in November 1943. Stalin perceived Overlord as the means of drawing off some of the German forces facing his advancing troops. His strategy was to end the war with his forces as far west as possible; Overlord would help, the Italian campaign would do nothing but hinder. Italy thus became the sideshow Churchill had feared.

From Teheran Churchill flew to Cairo for further discussions with Roosevelt and then on to Tunisia to see General Dwight Eisenhower, the Supreme Allied Commander, Mediterranean. As the War Cabinet had feared, Churchill's travels were taking their toll and in

Tunisia he developed pneumonia and a heart problem sufficiently serious for specialists to be flown in from Cairo and Italy. For a fortnight Churchill worked and received visitors from his bed. On Christmas Eve and Christmas Day he got up for conferences, which he attended in his silk damask dragon dressing gown, and then flew to Marrakech for 18 days of mixed convalescence and work. The battleship *King George V* brought him home to Plymouth and the King's train took him to London where, two hours after arriving, he was answering questions in Parliament.

On 6 June 1944 – D-Day – the Allies landed in Normandy. Churchill was planning to be present and had suggested to King George VI that they cross together but, when the King expressed fears for his Prime Minister's safety, reluctantly abandoned the idea. He crossed six days later in a destroyer and went ashore. He then cruised the shoreline and watched the Mulberry harbours being put in place. These artificial harbours, consisting of caissons towed across the Channel, owed something in their design to Churchill's instructions three years before which had ended 'don't argue the difficulties'. Finally back aboard the destroyer he requested she bombard the enemy.

In the earlier part of 1944 General Brooke had noted in his diary that he found Churchill 'desperately tired' and thought he was 'losing ground rapidly'. By June, perhaps from the stimulus of D-Day, he had regained his energy

and his humour. The German V1s, flying bombs or 'doodlebugs' as they became known, were now falling on London. Dictating a telegram to Roosevelt, Churchill broke the thread of argument to interject, 'At this moment a flying bomb is approaching this dwelling'. Then a little later concluded, 'Bomb has fallen some way off'.

On 20 July Churchill again visited the Normandy Front, spending three nights aboard a light cruiser before flying back to England. He took off again on 5 August for France but his aircraft was recalled much against his own inclinations when the one preceding it crashed in fog on landing, killing all occupants. Five

From left to right: The Earl of Athlone, Roosevelt, Churchill and Canadian Prime Minister Mackenzie King at the second Quebec Conference, September 1944, at which strategy for the rest of the war was decided.

Below: *Churchill sets foot on the east bank of the River Rhine shortly after it had been secured by Allied Forces, 24 March 1945.*

Opposite: *Churchill, Field Marshal Sir Alan Brooke and Field Marshal Sir Bernard Montgomery picnic on the west bank of the Rhine, 25 March 1945.*

General Sir Bernard Montgomery
(Field Marshal the Viscount Montgomery of Alamein)

The son of an Ulster clergyman, Bernard Montgomery was born in 1887. Commissioned into the infantry he was severely wounded in the opening battles of the First World War by the end of which he had become a lieutenant colonel. A teetotaler and non-smoker, a professional soldier to his finger tips and an outstanding trainer of troops, he had progressed to major general by the outbreak of the Second World War, when he distinguished himself in the confusion of the retreat to Dunkirk. Promoted to lieutenant general he was then placed in command of the defences of Southern England in anticipation of a German invasion.

In August 1942 Churchill appointed him to command the British 8th Army which had been severely mauled at the hands of the German Afrika Korps under Field Marshal Rommel. Within a few weeks General Montgomery had restored morale and in November 1942 he defeated Rommel at the Battle of El Alamein and thereafter pursued the German and Italian armies across North Africa to their final surrender in Tunisia in May 1943. He then shared major responsibility for the invasion of Sicily and the campaign through Italy.

Called home to command all ground forces during the allied invasion of North West Europe in June 1944 he subsequently, under General Eisenhower, led 21st Army Group through France, the Low Countries and Northern Germany, finally receiving the surrender of the German armed forces on 4 May 1945 on Luneburg Heath.

Montgomery's innate characteristics of egotism and tactlessness led to numerous personal conflicts with American senior commanders who were often exasperated with his insistence on complete readiness of both men and materiel before an attack. It was a policy born of his experience in the First World War and the knowledge that by 1944 Britain was fast running out of manpower. But it was a policy which brought success and endeared him to his troops.

After the war he commanded the British Army of the Rhine, became Chief of the Imperial General Staff, Chairman of the Defence Organisation of the Western European Union and, finally, Deputy Commander NATO.

days later Churchill flew to Italy. There were high-level conferences including not only the senior military commanders in the Mediterranean but also Marshal Tito of Yugoslavia. Churchill visited the front line in Italy and from a destroyer watched the invasion of the South of France. Describing the end of a conference on 21 August, Harold Macmillan wrote, 'all but Winston completely exhausted'. He was, perhaps, more tired than he appeared for, flying home on 29 August, he was taken ill. It was pneumonia again, necessitating several days in bed.

Still feeling unwell he boarded the *Queen Mary* on 5 September bound for America to

confer with Roosevelt. The following month Churchill decided that various problems concerned with the post-war shape of Europe required a face-to-face meeting in Moscow with Stalin. In November he was in Paris at the invitation of General de Gaulle and was moved to tears by the tremendous welcome from what seemed like the entire population lining the Champs Elysées.

Churchill was 70 on 30 November. But there could be no let up. Communism in Greece, with the possibility of civil war, ruined a family Christmas. Churchill landed at Athens in the afternoon of Christmas Day. Fighting was in progress between Greek government forces and Communists as he drove to the naval base where he boarded HMS *Ajax*. The following morning the ship was straddled by shellfire and a shell burst close to the craft taking Churchill ashore where, his Colt revolver in hand, he was taken by armoured car to the British Embassy. As he approached the Embassy two people were killed by machine gun bullets, some of which struck a building above his head. He was back in London by 5.00pm on the 29 December. He finally went to bed at 4.00am on the 30th having spent most of the night coercing the King of Greece into accepting a provisional government under the regency of Archbishop Damaskinos.

During the first week in February 1945, with the war in Europe approaching the end, the 'Big Three' met at Yalta in the Crimea to discuss the outline of post-war Europe. Churchill's party travelled in three aircraft, one of which crashed, killing 14 of the 19 people on board. Yalta was a frustrating time for Churchill. Roosevelt felt he had the measure of Stalin who throughout the conference played on the President's inclination to conciliate whenever deadlock threatened. History has vindicated Churchill, who wanted a far more robust dialogue with Stalin, but at the time, with Britain's reserves reduced almost to vanishing point, he could do no more than plead what he knew was the right course. But eloquence was not enough in the face of his need not to fall out with Roosevelt.

From Yalta Churchill went to Athens. On his previous visit a civil war had been raging. Now, six weeks later, as Churchill drove with

Anthony Eden
1st Earl of Avon

Anthony Eden is today remembered mainly for his role as Prime Minister during the Suez Crisis of 1956 but before that he had a long and distinguished career in the service of Britain.

Born in 1897, he was still at Eton at the outbreak of the First World War. Joining the King's Royal Rifle Corps in 1915, he fought in France where he was awarded the Military Cross. He entered politics in 1923, became Under-Secretary at the Foreign Office in 1932 and Lord Privy Seal and Minister for the League of Nations in Ramsay MacDonald's Government in 1931. Strongly anti-war, Eden sought to preserve peace through the League of Nations but recognised that it could not be maintained through the appeasement of Nazi Germany. Promoted to Foreign Secretary in 1935 he resigned from the cabinet in 1938 when the Prime Minister, Neville Chamberlain, conducted negotiations with Mussolini behind his back.

On the outbreak of the Second World War Eden was recalled to Chamberlain's cabinet as Secretary of State for Dominion Affairs. When Churchill became Prime Minister Eden was first appointed Secretary of State for War and then, a few months later, Foreign Secretary.

When the war ended it became clear that Churchill was far from retirement and Eden was left as his heir apparent. He became Foreign Secretary for the third time when the Conservatives returned to government in 1951. He was again seriously ill and was out of action through much of 1953. This was the year in which Churchill suffered a severe stroke but, in a manner unimaginable today, this was concealed from the public and he recovered to take up the reins again until he finally retired in 1955.

Eden was past his best by the time he became Prime Minister in April 1955. In 1956 after Gamal Abdel Nasser, President of Egypt, nationalised the Suez Canal, Britain and France invaded Egypt. Britain was still, in the wake of the Second World War, financially dependent on America and in the face of pressure from President Eisenhower Eden was forced to withdraw British troops.

The Suez fiasco led to a further breakdown in Eden's health and he resigned as Prime Minister in the following year. He died in 1977.

Triumph – this time the famous V-sign really means, 'We've won!'

The Potsdam Conference of July 1945, attended by Churchill, Truman and Stalin, was intended to establish the political framework of post-war Europe. In fact, the conflict of interest that emerged between Russia and the other Allies marked the beginning of the Cold War.

the Regent, Archbishop Damaskinos, into Constitution Square, it was packed with cheering crowds. After dinner at the British Embassy, Churchill took off for Egypt. Roosevelt had preceded him there and the two men said farewell for what turned out to be the last time on 15 February on board the USS *Quincy*, in Alexandria harbour.

Returning to London from Germany on 6 March, Churchill decided to be with Field Marshal General Montgomery when the British troops crossed the Rhine. He flew out on 23 March and crossed the river two days later. Travelling along the bank by road he was well within range of German artillery and he

came under shellfire while inspecting the wrecked railway bridge at Wesel.

The end of the war was in sight when Churchill wrote to Roosevelt of the need for the British and American forces to advance as fast and as far to the east as possible. Having warned of Russian political intentions he concluded, 'I therefore consider that from a political standpoint we should march as far east into Germany as possible, and that should Berlin be in our grasp we should certainly take it'. But the American strategy driving the advance into Germany reflected the earlier arguments which had arisen over the Italian campaign and took no account of the strategic implications for post-war Europe. It saw no merit in Churchill's argument. It accepted at face value Stalin's declaration that Berlin was of no strategic importance and that he had allocated only secondary forces to advance on it. That was far from the truth.

Roosevelt, who had looked frail throughout the Yalta conference, was ailing fast and would die on 12 April. The Vice-President, Harry Truman, became President.

Victory in Europe was celebrated on the night of 8 May, the instruments of surrender having come into force at midnight. For Churchill the celebrations were overshadowed by events in Eastern Europe where he anticipated a showdown with Stalin over the sovereignty of countries occupied by Russian troops.

There had been no General Election in

A French worker lights Churchill's cigar, Cherbourg, July 1944.

Britain for ten years but Churchill had hoped to maintain the Coalition Government until Japan was defeated. However the Labour Party wished otherwise and polling day was set for 5 July. Meanwhile Churchill formed a Caretaker Government and prepared for the final 'Big Three' conference scheduled for mid-July in Potsdam.

Voting in the General Election took place in Britain on 5 July but, as there were many hundreds of thousands of votes to come in from the forces abroad, the result was still unknown when Churchill flew to Potsdam on 15 July for the conference which was to settle the outline of post-war Europe. The Potsdam Conference was, like Yalta, both frustrating and disappointing for Churchill. Stalin began with a winning hand. His forces had rampaged westwards occupying the territories over which he sought control and he had no intention of withdrawing. Truman was unaccustomed to negotiating at this level and, anyway, more concerned with the war in the Pacific. Stalin went back on his word and did not accept arrangements thought to have been agreed at Yalta. The conference adjourned halfway through for Churchill and Attlee, his former deputy and Leader of the Opposition, to return to London for the election results. There were a lot of loose ends left to be tied up when the conference resumed: such contentious subjects as the Polish borders and German coal for Russia in exchange for food. Churchill was

determined that, on Poland at least, he would hold out when he returned to the conference table.

In Britain Churchill was supremely popular. He was cheered spontaneously wherever he went. This was a tribute to Churchill the war leader, entirely disassociated with Churchill the leader of the Conservative Party which the working class thought had failed them in pre-war days. They wanted a party sympathetic to the worker and for them that was Labour. Churchill's commitment as a Liberal to social reform was too far in the past. Churchill had never been a committed party politician and the years as wartime leader had not increased his appetite for party politics. During the election campaign before Potsdam he had done no good to the Conservative cause when he likened Socialism, his invariable description of Labour policy, to totalitarianism and declared it would need to rely on 'some form of Gestapo'. This wild exaggeration drew a hugely unfavourable response but the Conservatives' cause was in any case lost as was seen when the votes were finally counted. The Conservatives had lost more than half their seats in Parliament. Labour had a clear majority and it was Attlee who returned to Potsdam to represent Britain.

Celebrating Victory in Europe with the Royal Family, on the balcony at Buckingham Palace, 8 May 1945.

Winston Churchill's Favourite Things

Once, in answer to a hotel manager's enquiry if all was well, Churchill said, 'I am a man of simple tastes, easily satisfied by the best'. The best is often the most expensive; therefore the Churchills' stretched finances were always on the brink of disaster.

He had always like Pol Roger champagne, but after meeting Odette Pol Roger he drank it almost exclusively, having a particular preference for the 1928 vintage. One of his unfulfilled desires was to visit 44 Avenue de Champagne, the Pol Rogers' château in Epernay, which he described as 'the world's most drinkable address' and to 'tread the grapes with his bare feet'. He even named one of his racehorses Pol Roger after his favourite champagne.

The Pol Roger family returned the compliment when, on his death, they added a black border to all bottles of the 'White Foil' sold in the United Kingdom. In 1990 this 'mourning' band was lightened to navy blue. In 1984 Pol Roger celebrated their most famous client by naming their prestige champagne 'Cuvée Sir Winston Churchill'.

He was rarely seen without his trademark Churchill Romeo y Julieta Havana cigar. He liked consommé, dover sole, fillet steak and ice cream. All meals were accompanied by fine wines and ended with brandy and cigars.

He had a great fondness for all living creatures and delighted in visiting and feeding the fish, the black swans and the pigs at Chartwell. He enjoyed the company of Rufus, his poodle, Jock, his marmalade cat, and Toby, his budgerigar. Above all, he liked to be surrounded by as many members of his family as possible. When not occupied with affairs of state he derived enormous pleasure from painting.

His favourite place was Chartwell, of which he said, 'A day away from Chartwell is a day wasted'.

1986
BRUT   BRUT
CHAMPAGNE
Pol Roger
12% vol   cl75d
A ÉPERNAY   FRANCE
PRODUCE OF FRANCE
ELABORÉ PAR POL ROGER, EPERNAY, FRANCE

PR
Pol Roger & Cie   *Pol Roger & Cie*
CUVÉE
SIR WINSTON CHURCHILL

CHAMPAGNE
EXTRA CUVÉE   RÉSE
BY APPOINTMENT
Pol Roger & Co
Epernay
RESERVED FOR
GREAT BRITAIN

11/27 LONDON 25/24 26 2316
POLROGER WON SPLENDIDLY TODAY SO THERE IS A SMALL
PROFIT FOR YOU ON BOTH RACES BEST LOVE = WINSTON +

T.L.G. 701   Pour tout renseignement concernant ce télégramme, s'adresser au bureau distributeur.   A B C D E

5

COLD WAR STATESMAN 1945–64

Clementine, recognising the strain under which her husband had laboured for six years and the enormity of the problems ahead, said of the election result, 'It may well be a blessing in disguise'. To which Churchill replied, 'At the moment it seems quite effectively disguised'. He was not ready to lay down the burdens of office.

Japan surrendered on 14 August 1945 and the Second World War was over. Churchill, in conversation with his secretary, Elizabeth Layton, was obviously sad at not being in at the end. At a loss for a reply, she suggested he should now rest awhile. His reply reflected the one he had given to Clementine. 'I wanted to do the peace too.' He wanted to show the world that he was not only a warrior but also a peacemaker.

Undoubtedly he was, as his record with South Africa and Ireland shows, but it is unlikely, as the Prime Minister of an impoverished post-war Britain over shadowed by America, that the world would have felt his impact as it had done in 1940. Indeed, the contribution he was to make in shaping world events in the immediate post-war years would almost certainly have been less notable had he

been burdened with the task of re-building Britain.

Churchill declined King George VI's offer of the Order of the Garter and remarked, 'How can I accept the Order of the Garter from the King when I have been given the order of the boot by the people?' Somewhat disappointed, the King conferred on him the Order of Merit. Eight years later, after some deliberation, Churchill would accept the Order of the Garter from Queen Elizabeth II.

With the war over, the family prescribed a painting holiday in Italy and the South of France. In addition to his paints he took with him printed and bound all the wartime minutes he had written to the Chiefs of Staff. It would seem that he had already decided to write the history of the recent war. It would have otherwise been quite out of character although at the time he was saying to his publishers that he was still undecided. In 1948 he would tell Parliament, 'I consider that it will be found much better by all parties to leave the past to history, especially as I propose to write that history myself'. By then the first volume of *The Second World War* was about to be published. In all there would be six volumes, the final one

1945 National Government General Election Poster.

appearing in 1954, in his 80th year. It was an astonishing historical and literary performance which, for the first time in his life, freed him from financial worry. But money had not driven the project. The history was written to establish his view of the war as the authorised version. In this the feckless Britain of the 1930s showed its true colours in 1940 when, alone, it held the ring while America awoke to the situation, thus permitting the Anglo-American alliance to triumph. It ends with the tragedy of a communist dominated Eastern Europe. The author's philosophy is epitomised in the moral of his enormous work, 'In war, resolution; in defeat, defiance; in victory, magnanimity; in peace, goodwill'.

At Yalta and before, Churchill had drawn attention to the potential for post-war tragedy, yet leaders of the Western World were ignoring it even as it was unfolding. In March 1946, Churchill shocked people into recognition of the facts. Returning from his painting holiday he found awaiting him an invitation from President Truman to speak at Westminster College, Fulton, Missouri. This small college of only 212 students in heartland America had contrived this coup through a Presidential contact. What no one realised at the time was the international significance of what they had set in motion, for Churchill's words at Fulton would define the international politics of the next four decades. The fact that Churchill was to be introduced by the President and that his speech on world affairs would be broadcast from coast to coast, had fuelled expectations. By mid-January the college had received some 15,000 requests for tickets. The 2,800 seats in the gymnasium and the 900 in the chapel had been reserved. Public address systems serving such places as the downtown churches and the courthouse square catered for the overflow. The basement of the gymnasium was fitted out to cope with some 400 pressmen.

Churchill entitled his speech 'The Sinews of Peace' but, through one of his memorable sentences, it immediately became known as the 'Iron Curtain' speech, 'From Stettin in the Baltic to Trieste in the Adriatic, an iron curtain has descended across the Continent'. He wished to reach an honest understanding with Russia but to do so required a resolve which was then lacking. His speech, warning of the Russian threat and calling for Anglo-American unity in meeting it, caused considerable waves throughout the world. In the war-weary West it received an almost universally hostile press. In London *The Times*, critical of Churchill's theme, thought

Churchill and President Truman set out for Fulton, Missouri, where on 5 March 1946 he gave the address entitled 'The Sinews of Peace', more commonly remembered as the 'Iron Curtain' speech. He had used the phrase some months earlier in a telegram to Truman, written a few days after VE Day. Referring to the fact that the Russian army showed no sign of disbanding, he said, 'an iron curtain is drawn down upon their front. We do not know what is going on behind'.

that democracy and communism 'had much to learn from one another'. The *Chicago Sun*, which a few days earlier had been keen to publish his earlier speeches, wrote of 'poisonous doctrines'. To the east, in Russia, *Pravda*'s headline ran 'Churchill Rattles the Sabre'. The President claimed, disingenuously, that he had not seen the contents beforehand. In Britain, Attlee felt obliged to emphasise that Churchill had expressed personal opinions. But within weeks the free world had awoken to the warning. Only nine months later Churchill was able to write to Governor Thomas Dewey of New York, 'If I made the Fulton speech today it would be criticised as consisting of platitudes'.

He had no shortage of platforms from which to proclaim his message. Institutions and universities were queuing up to honour him, each one requiring a speech. On one such occasion he joked, 'No one ever passed so few examinations and received so many degrees'.

It was not only an Anglo-American shield which Churchill advocated. He also saw the need for a European alliance. In November 1945, even before Fulton, he had called for a 'United States of Europe' when addressing the Belgian Senate. Only six months after the end of the European war his mind was already set on the measures needed to prevent anything so terrible happening again. In September 1946, at the University of Zurich, he set out his vision of a United States of Europe, the first step towards which would be the reconciliation of France and Germany. He saw Russia as a potential partner, not in permanent hostility. Almost two years later, in May 1948 at the inaugural meeting of the Congress of Europe, he spoke of the need to 'efface frontiers' and to

Cap d'Ai, Alpes-Maritimes.

Painting had been a source of relaxation to Churchill since the First World War. He expressed his hope for the afterlife, 'When I get to heaven I want to spend the first million years in painting and so get to the bottom of the subject'.

In 1950 Churchill returned to the island of Madeira for the first time since he called there on his way to South Africa in 1899. Here he is painting at the fishing port of Cámara dos Lobos.

restore the economic life of Germany. In Brussels in February 1949 he spoke in favour of a European Court of Human Rights and in August pressed successfully for the inclusion of Germany in the Council of Europe. In 1950 Churchill argued for the creation of a European army as the only way of persuading Europe to integrate German forces in its defence but, although he did not say so at the time, did not intend Britain to join it.

At the beginning of the 21st century the political circumstances are quite different from those which prompted Churchill's far-sighted views on Europe and one can only guess what his attitude would be to the European Union as we know it today. He certainly saw Britain with a different role to that of other European nations. He would not under any circum-stances allow our ties with Europe to weaken our close relationship with the United States. There was also the Commonwealth about which Churchill had said in 1949, ' We shall never do anything to weaken the ties of blood, of sentiment, and tradition and common interests which unite us with the other members of the British family of nations'. It was as if there were three overlapping circles, Europe, the Commonwealth and the United States with Britain in the privileged position of being the only one with a place in each. It may have been a legacy of Churchill's roots in Victorian Britain, but he undoubtedly felt that Britain's position was beneficial to the others.

Unlike present day politicians he could trade on Britain's and the Commonwealth's crucial role in a recent world war.

While Churchill had been devoting his energies to world affairs and writing *The Second World War*, his parliamentary colleagues had become uneasy about his party leadership. They felt he was giving too little attention to it. In 1949 he took Clementine's advice and cancelled a holiday in Jamaica with Lord Beaverbrook when she wrote, 'I do not mind if you resign the leadership when things are good, but I can't bear you to be accepted murmuringly and uneasily'.

Churchill would remain in power as Leader of the Opposition and then Prime Minister for another six years after Clementine's warning. It was not simply the power alone which attracted him but the genuine feeling that with his wealth of experience he could, more than anyone else, resolve the dangers of the Cold War. In 1951 a general election returned the Conservative Party to power with an overall majority and he was Prime Minister again. In November that year he was 77 and confided to his Principal Private Secretary, Jock Colville, that he intended to remain in office for just one more year before handing over to Anthony Eden.

In the New Year of 1952 Churchill landed from the *Queen Mary* in New York en route to meet President Truman. At sea he had been reluctant to read his briefing material, telling

Colville that he was going to the United States to 're-establish relations, not to conduct business'. He again addressed Congress, speaking of the benefits arising from 'the fraternal association of the United States with Britain and the Commonwealth, and the new unity growing up in Europe'.

Shortly after Churchill's return from America in January 1952, the death of King George VI and the accession of Queen Elizabeth II caused a pause in domestic politics, but thereafter the pace picked up and the immense amount of governmental work covering affairs at home and abroad and the anxieties of the Cold War was a heavy load for a man of 77.

Prime Minister Churchill at the Cabinet Table, 1955.

The burdens of office were beginning to show. In June 1952 members of his government asked him to set a date for his resignation but with the election in the United States of Eisenhower as President, Churchill saw the chance to use his authority and reputation in reconciling America and Russia. Resignation was out of the question.

Meeting Eisenhower in January 1953, Churchill urged that they should both go to Moscow but Eisenhower declined. In March Stalin died, opening the chance of dialogue with his successors, but once more the President refused to become involved. In May, Bermuda was agreed as the venue for a summit between the President and Prime Minister, but in June a serious stroke intervened and Churchill was faced with a long recovery. The press were informed only that he was in need of a complete rest.

By early October Churchill had recovered sufficiently to impress the Conservative Party conference with a 50-minute speech which dispelled the party rumours that he was finished and dashed Eden's hopes of stepping into Churchill's shoes at an early date. In mid-October Churchill was awarded the Nobel Prize for Literature and in early November his performance re-established him in Parliament where, so closely had the secret been guarded, none had realised how serious his illness had been. *The Times* wrote of his 'complete authority over the Commons'. The postponed

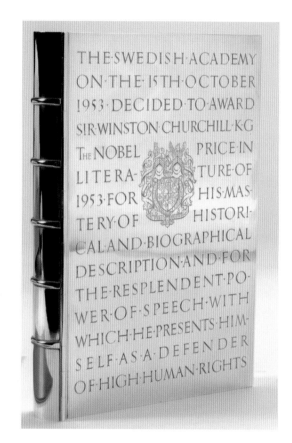

conference with Eisenhower which took place in December covered a wide range of subjects on none of which was there an easy meeting of minds. Eisenhower's bellicose attitude towards Russia was at odds with Churchill's hope for *détente*. Churchill saw no contradiction between a strong defence against potential aggression and attempts to create conditions for peaceful coexistence, but his advocacy failed to persuade the United States of the

benefits of a common approach to Russia in order to achieve a summit conference.

In June 1954, Churchill went again to the United States. He and Eisenhower announced their agreement that Western Germany should take its place as an equal partner in the defence of the West, thus fulfilling Churchill's plea at Zurich eight years before. Eisenhower seemed to have softened his approach to Russia and during this conference agreed to a meeting with the Russians and also to a

preliminary visit to Moscow by Churchill. But Churchill's proposed visit floundered in the face of Cabinet opposition.

Still Churchill clung to office, irritated by speculation in Parliament about his resignation. In December he wrote to Eisenhower that he still hoped 'we may reach a top level meeting with the new regime in Russia and that you and I may both be present'. But it was not to be and after a number of false starts, galling in the extreme to Eden, Churchill

Left: *Churchill holds the door for the Queen as she and Prince Philip leave Downing Street after having dinner with Winston and Clementine, 4 April 1955.*

Opposite: *Sketch by Graham Sutherland for a portrait commissioned by the House of Commons to celebrate Churchill's 80th birthday. Churchill liked the sketches, but hated the finished portrait. He thought it made him look old and hard. Clementine was furious with Sutherland and had it destroyed after Churchill's death.*

eventually stepped down on 5 April 1955. The Queen said that she believed he wished to continue in the House of Commons otherwise she would offer him a Dukedom. He replied that he would like to go on in the Commons while he felt physically fit but that if he felt the work was too hard he would be proud if she chose to reconsider her proposal. He would continue to represent the constituency of Epping to within six months of his death.

Six days later he set off with Clementine and his easel for a fortnight in Sicily. The weather was indifferent and he only painted two dull canvases, however he had already begun to revise the 1939 proofs of *A History of The English Speaking Peoples*.

In 1956, in response to the seizure of the Suez Canal by President Nasser of Egypt, Britain, France and Israel invaded Egypt. Churchill issued a press statement supporting

Top: Churchill's banner as a Knight of the Garter, a duplicate of the one that hung in St George's Chapel, Windsor, has pride of place in his study at Chartwell.

Churchill's orders, decorations and medals. As a young man, Churchill was accused of being a 'medal hunter'. In fact, he received most of these awards after the Second World War. He declined the Queen's offer of a Dukedom, declaring that he did not want to retire in a 'blaze of honours'. Three honours are not shown here because they were returned after Churchill's death to the monarchs who had awarded them.

Left: *April 1955: the news reaches the British public that their 80-year old 'elder statesman' is to retire.*

he was again returned as their Member of Parliament at the General Election in October, the last election he would contest. On 27 July 1964 he went to the House of Commons for the last time where a very large crowd gathered outside to witness the departure of the great parliamentarian who had served there under six monarchs.

CHARTWELL

We used to spend quite long periods at Chartwell. In the same way as my grandfather went to Blenheim, we would go with our nanny to Chartwell in the school holidays. The best moments were our walks with Grandpapa and Rufus, his brown poodle. He loved animals, so after visiting the pigs and the black swans we would always end up feeding the fish. He believed they really recognised him because when he threw the food in, they all came up to the surface. He loved being at Chartwell with his family around him.

I remember my grandfather as a relaxed person, which seems strange, but on the whole I saw him at home, when he was enjoying himself – either entertaining friends, or painting, or visiting animals. Our life with him was one of simple pleasures which we could all enjoy, regardless of our different ages and experiences.

Celia Sandys

the action of the Eden government. He was then taken aback when the operation was abruptly called off as a result of American pressure and became deeply concerned at the consequent rupture of Anglo-American relations. To his Private Secretary, Anthony Montague Browne, Churchill observed, 'I'd have never done it without squaring the Americans and once I'd started I would never have dared stop'.

Churchill now spent more time in the sun, usually the South of France, returning to Britain to attend occasional parliamentary debates. In 1959 he crossed the Atlantic once again to see Eisenhower. In September that year he spoke in his constituency from which

Opposite: *Churchill looking out over the grounds of Chartwell.*

Overleaf: *Churchill's State Funeral, 30 January 1965.*

EPILOGUE

My grandfather lived out the last years of his life at a slower and slower pace. Once out of office it seemed that his incredible zest for life, which had already diminished with time, was ebbing away.

He still derived pleasure from painting of which he had written: 'Happy are the painters, for they shall not be lonely. Light and colour, peace and hope, will keep them company to the end or almost to the end of the day.' So it was for him and he continued painting until his late eighties. Even after he had put his paints away for the last time he still enjoyed holidays in the South of France and cruising in the Mediterranean.

On November 30 1949, his seventy-fifth birthday, speaking at Mansion House he had said: 'I am prepared to meet my Maker, whether my Maker is prepared for the great ordeal of meeting me is another matter.'

Fifteen years later we celebrated his ninetieth birthday. The unspoken thought in all our minds that that meeting would not be long delayed. Six weeks later it seemed that the inevitable was about to happen. He had once predicted that he would die on the anniversary of his father's death. The country braced itself, the family prepared for the end, the patient slumbered on, his faithful marmalade cat at his side.

Early on the morning of January 24 1965 it was clear that the end was near. We gathered round his bed to say good bye. Seventy years to the day and almost to the minute since Lord Randolph had died Winston Churchill slipped imperceptibly away to meet his maker.

Plans for a funeral code-named 'Operation Hope Not', had been in place some years but, in the meantime, there was to be a chance for the people to say goodbye to the man who had served his country and six monarchs so faithfully. More than 300,000 queued for hours along the Embankment, in the freezing cold, to file past his coffin at his lying-in-state in Westminster Hall.

On 30 January grief-stricken crowds lined the route that the procession would take for the first state funeral for a commoner since Gladstone's in 1898. The family gathered at Westminster Hall, from where the men followed the gun carriage, which bore the coffin, on foot and the women rode in carriages from the Royal Mews. My sister and I were in the second carriage behind my grandmother and my aunts. As we slowly made our way along Whitehall past the Cenotaph and the government buildings that had played such a part in our Grandfather's life we were so close to the grieving crowds, some openly weeping, some ashen faced, that if we had stretched out our hands we could have touched them.

The service in St Paul's Cathedral was both moving and triumphant with all Grandpapa's favourite hymns. The Queen, the Royal Family and all the visiting Heads of State stood on the steps of the Cathedral to say their final farewell. We followed the gun carriage to Tower Pier for the journey up the Thames to Waterloo Station and the train which would carry him to his final resting place.

As the *Havengore* began its short journey there was a roaring sound overhead as fighter planes from the Royal Air Force flew past in perfect formation. In silent contrast to this, the cranes along the embankment dipped their heads in salute.

We buried him at Bladon next to his parents and within sight of Blenheim Palace where he had been born 90 years before.

The union flag that was draped over Churchill's coffin as his body lay in state in Westminster Hall. He had helped to plan his own funeral, 'Operation Hope Not', in the 1950s. Queen Elizabeth II ordered a State Funeral, the first monarch ever to attend the funeral of a commoner. Churchill had been the first Prime Minister of her reign.

CHRONOLOGY

1874 30 November 1874, born at Blenheim Palace.

1888 Enters Harrow School.

1893 Enters Royal Military Academy, Sandhurst.

1895 Commissioned into 4th Hussars. Takes leave to observe guerrilla war in Cuba.

1896 India, to Bangalore with 4th Hussars.

1897 India, to north-west frontier, attached to Malakand Field Force during tribal war.

1898 Sudan, attached to 21st Lancers. Takes part in last regimental cavalry charge at Omdurman.

1899 Resigns from army. Fails at first attempt to be elected to Parliament. Goes to South Africa as war correspondent for *Morning Post* to cover Boer War. Captured and escapes. Commissioned into the South African Light Horse.

1900 July, returns to England. October, elected to Parliament as a Conservative.

1904 Breaks with Conservative Party, joins Liberals.

1905 Under Secretary of State for the Colonies.

1908 President of the Board of Trade. Marries Clementine Hozier.

1910 Home Secretary.

1911 Siege of Sidney Street. First Lord of the Admiralty.

1914 The First World War begins.

1915 Resigns from Cabinet following failure of Dardanelles campaign. Rejoins army. To France, with Grenadier Guards.

1916 Appointed to command 6th Battalion Royal Scots Fusiliers. Returns to London, resigns from army and resumes political career.

1917 Minister of Munitions.

1918 November, war ends.

1919 Secretary of State for War and Air.

1921 Colonial Secretary.

1922 Loses seat in General Election.

1924 Breaks with Liberal Party. Re-elected to Parliament as Conservative. Chancellor of the Exchequer.

1930s 'Wilderness Years'. Out of office. Warns against danger from Nazi Germany.

1939 September, Britain declares war on Germany. First Lord of the Admiralty again.

1940 10 May, becomes Prime Minister.

1941 Atlantic Charter.
Meeting with Franklin D. Roosevelt. December, Pearl Harbor. Britain declares war on Japan. Germany and Italy declare war on US.

1942 Meeting with Stalin in Moscow.

1943 Casablanca and Teheran conferences.

1945 Yalta and Potsdam conferences.
May, victory in Europe.
Government defeated in general election. Churchill stands down as Prime Minister.

1946 'Iron Curtain' speech, at Fulton, Missouri.

1951 Prime Minister again.

1953 Nobel Prize for Literature.

1955 April, resigns as Prime Minister.

1963 Granted honorary American Citizenship.

1964 Leaves the House of Commons.

1965 24 January, dies in London.

THE CHURCHILL FAMILY TREE

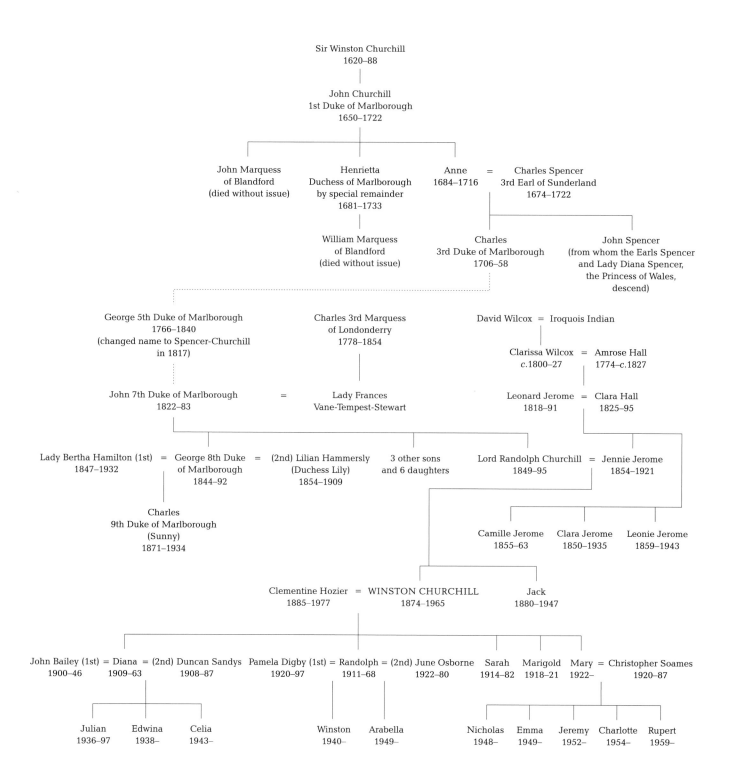

Sir Winston Churchill
1620–88

John Churchill
1st Duke of Marlborough
1650–1722

John Marquess
of Blandford
(died without issue)

Henrietta
Duchess of Marlborough
by special remainder
1681–1733

Anne
1684–1716 = Charles Spencer
3rd Earl of Sunderland
1674–1722

William Marquess
of Blandford
(died without issue)

Charles
3rd Duke of Marlborough
1706–58

John Spencer
(from whom the Earls Spencer
and Lady Diana Spencer,
the Princess of Wales,
descend)

George 5th Duke of Marlborough
1766–1840
(changed name to Spencer-Churchill
in 1817)

Charles 3rd Marquess
of Londonderry
1778–1854

David Wilcox = Iroquois Indian

Clarissa Wilcox = Amrose Hall
c.1800–27 1774–c.1827

John 7th Duke of Marlborough
1822–83 = Lady Frances
Vane-Tempest-Stewart

Leonard Jerome = Clara Hall
1818–91 1825–95

Lady Bertha Hamilton (1st) = George 8th Duke = (2nd) Lilian Hammersly
1847–1932 of Marlborough (Duchess Lily)
1844–92 1854–1909

3 other sons
and 6 daughters

Lord Randolph Churchill = Jennie Jerome
1849–95 1854–1921

Charles
9th Duke of Marlborough
(Sunny)
1871–1934

Camille Jerome
1855–63

Clara Jerome
1850–1935

Leonie Jerome
1859–1943

Clementine Hozier = WINSTON CHURCHILL
1885–1977 1874–1965

Jack
1880–1947

John Bailey (1st) = Diana = (2nd) Duncan Sandys
1900–46 1909–63 1908–87

Pamela Digby (1st) = Randolph = (2nd) June Osborne
1920–97 1911–68 1922–80

Sarah
1914–82

Marigold
1918–21

Mary = Christopher Soames
1922– 1920–87

Julian
1936–97

Edwina
1938–

Celia
1943–

Winston
1940–

Arabella
1949–

Nicholas
1948–

Emma
1949–

Jeremy
1952–

Charlotte
1954–

Rupert
1959–

Churchill in 1899, during
his time as a war
correspondent in South
Africa for the Morning Post.

BIBLIOGRAPHY

Balsan, Consuelo Vanderbilt. *The Glitter and the Gold*, Heinemann, 1953.

Best, Geoffrey. *Churchill, A Study in Greatness*, Hambeldon & London, 2001.

Bonham Carter, Violet. *Winston Churchill As I Knew Him,* Eyre & Spottiswoode, 1965.

Chaplin, E D W. *Winston Churchill and Harrow*, Harrow School Bookshop, 1941.

Churchill, John Spencer, *A Crowded Canvas*, Odhams, 1961.

Churchill, Randolph S. *Winston S. Churchill*, Vols I & II, Heinemann, 1966 & 67.

Churchill, Randolph S. *Companion, Vols I & II*, 1966.

Churchill, Sarah. *A Thread in the Tapestry*, André Deutsch, 1967.

Churchill, Sarah. *Keep on Dancing*, Weidenfeld and Nicolson, 1981.

Churchill, Winston S. *London to Ladysmith*, Longmans, Green & Co, 1900.

Churchill, Winston S. *Ian Hamilton's March*, Longmans, Green & Co, 1900.

Churchill, Winston S. *My Early Life*, Macmillan 1930.

Churchill, Winston S. *Thoughts and Adventures*, Thornton Butterworth, 1932.

Churchill, Winston S. *The Second World War*, Vols I – VI, 1948–54.

Churchill, Winston S. *Painting as a Pastime*, Odhams Press Ltd, 1948.

Churchill, Winston S. *His Father's Son*, Weidenfeld & Nicolson, 1996

Clifford, Clark. *Counsel to the President*, Random House, New York, 1991.

Colville, John. *The Fringes of Power,*

Gilbert, Martin. *Winston S Churchill, Vols III – VIII*, Heinemann, 1971–88

Gilbert, Martin. *Churchill A Life,* Heinemann, 1991.

Graebner, Walter. *My Dear Mr Churchill*, Michael Joseph, 1965.

Graham, Stewart. *Burying Caesar*, Weidenfeld & Nicolson, 1999.

Halle, Kay. *Irrepressible Churchill,* Cleveland World Publishing Company, 1966.

Jenkins, Roy. *Churchill*, Macmillian, 2001.

Lukacs, John. *5 Days in London May 1940*, Yale University Press, 1999.

Moir, Phyllis. *I was Winston Churchill's Private Secretary*, W Funk, 1961.

Montague Browne, Anthony. *Long Sunset*, Cassell Publishers Ltd, 1995.

Moran, Lord. *Churchill the Struggle for Survival*, Constable & Company, 1966.

Nel, Elizabeth. *Mr Churchill's Secretary*, Hodder & Stoughton, 1958.

Pilpel, Robert H. *Churchill in America*, Harcourt Brace Jovanovich, 1976.

Pakenham, Thomas. *The Boer War*, Weidenfeld & Nicolson, 1979.

Pawle, Gerald. *The War and Colonel Warden*, George Harrap & Co Ltd, 1963.

Roberts, Andrew. *The Holy Fox*, Weidenfeld & Nicolson 1991.

Sandys, Celia. *From Winston with Love & Kisses*, Sinclair–Stevenson, 1994.

Sandys, Celia. *Churchill Wanted Dead or Alive*, HarperCollins, 1999.

Soames, Mary. *Clementine*, Cassell Ltd, 1979.

Soames, Mary. *Winston Churchill: His Life as a Painter*, William Collins Sons & Co, 1990.

Soames, Mary. *Speaking for Themselves*, Doubleday, 1998.

Thompson, W H. *I was Churchill's Shadow*, Christopher Johnson, 1951.

ACKNOWLEDGEMENTS

I am very grateful to all those who have allowed me to use material to which they own the copyright, most particularly, my aunt Mary Soames and my cousin Winston S Churchill. My thanks go to Allen Packwood and his team at The Churchill Archives Centre, Churchill College, Cambridge for all the help they have given. Also to Minnie Churchill and Anthea Morton Saner.

I want to thank Andrew Roberts and Terry Charman for very kindly sparing the time to read and comment on the manuscript.

As always I am extremely grateful to my husband, Ken Perkins.

Celia Sandys

The Publisher would like to thank the following for their kind assistance with the research and production of the book.

Patrick Kinna
Elizabeth Nell
George Elsey
Captain Shaw
The Lady Soames, DBE
Butler & Tanner

Many thanks to all of the individuals and institutions who have supplied images and granted us permission to use them in this book.

CREDITS

Imperial War Museum: 6 (HU 87398), 15 (ZZZ 7555D), 17 (HU 90489), 19 (ZZZ 5426F), 24 (ZZZ 007150), 32 (Q 113382), 34 (Q 42037), 35 (HU53847), 39 (O 30452), 45 (CP 7529D), 46 (Q 84076), 47 (Q 84077), 51 (Q 49305), (Q 11429), 57 (HU 81615), 78 (LD 6217), 85 (H 3514), 86 (HU 90343), 88 (CP 8705), 90 (H 2628), 91 (*left:* PST 0736), 92 (*left:* PST 8774; *right:* PST 0761), 93 (*left:* PST 3363; *right:* PST 3107), 94 (HU 87398), 95 (HU 1135), 96 (H 8863), 97 (*top:* HU 63613; *bottom:* PST 8775), 98 (H 4961), 99 (*top:* LD 4589, *bottom:* H 39498), 100 (H 4367), 104 (H 16643), 107 (H 16478), 108 (H 12739), 109 (H 12752), 111 (A 16710), 113 (NYP 54898), 116 (E 15299), 117 (CAN 846), 119 (EA 26941), 121 (TR 1347), 122 (BU 2249), 123 (BU 2636), 124 (TR 2828), 126 (BU 9195), 127 (PL 65765), 128 (OWIL 30645), 129 (MH 21835), 132 (PST 8449), 148–149 (R 33301).

Getty: 18, 21, 26 (*left*), 30, 36, 37, 52, 55, 62, 65, 67, 68, 75, 79, 80, 135, 141, 142,

Magnum Photos/Philippe Halsman: 147

AKG: 23, 49, 110, 115, 139,

Popperfoto: 58, 59, 138, 146

Broadwater: 8, 10 (*left*; *top right*), 11 (*right*), 13, 14, 22, 25 (*top right*), 26 (*right*), 27, 28, 35 (*left*; *right*), 40, 41 (*left*; *middle*), 43, 44, 51 (*top*), 60, 61 (*top*; *bottom*), 70, 71, 74, 77, 81, 137,

National Trust, Chartwell: 11 (*left*), 41 (*right*), 63 (*top*), 141 (*top*), 103 (*far right*),

Lent by the National Trust, Chartwell, by permission of The Lady Soames DBE: 136

Queen's Royal Hussars: 20 (*top*)

Churchill Heritage: 72, 73, 132

Mr Winston S Churchill: 10 (*bottom right*), 25 (*top left*), 50 (*top*), 63 (*middle*), 140, 144, 145 (*bottom left*; *bottom right*), 151

Churchill Papers, Churchill Archives Centre, Mr Winston S Churchill: 12, 15 (*left*),

Churchill Papers, Churchill Archives Centre, with the permission of Her Majesty Queen Elizabeth II: 77 (*left*), 118

Baroness Spencer-Churchill Collection, Churchill Archives Centre: 40 (*right:* CSCT 01/001/3), 48 (WCHL 04/018), 101 (CSCT 01/024/1-3)

Harrow School: 16

Hills & Saunders, Harrow (song): 17

Harlan R Crow Library: 25 (*bottom*)

Punch Ltd: 32 (*top right*)

Gallery Oldham: 32 (*bottom right*)

Douglas Hall: 38

Mr Dewar Gibb: 50 (*bottom*)

The National Archives: 63 (*bottom*)

The Prime Minister's Office: 83

Sir David Low and *The Evening Standard*: 89

Mr Tony Woodhead: 134

National Portrait Gallery, London: 143

INDEX